ACTS

A Devotional Commentary

D0062562

ACTS

A Devotional Commentary

Meditations on the Acts of the Apostles

GENERAL EDITOR
Leo Zanchettin

the WORD
among us

Library
Benedictine University Mesa

The Word Among Us Press
9639 Doctor Perry Road
Ijamsville, Maryland 21754
www.wau.org
ISBN: 0-932085-52-0

Scripture quotations are from the Revised Standard Version of the Bible, © 1946, 1952, 1971, by the Division of Christian Education of the National Council of the Churches of Christ in the U.S.A. Used by permission.

Cover Art:
Titian, Pentecost, S. Maria della Salute, Venice, Italy
Art Resource, New York, NY

Cover design by David Crosson

Made and printed in the United States of America.

Foreword

Dear Friends in Christ:

Not long after Pentecost Sunday, St. Peter cried out, "Repent therefore, and turn to God so that your sins may be wiped out, so that times of refreshing may come from the presence of the Lord" (Acts 3:19-20). With these few words, Peter summarized the heart of the gospel message, and the heart of the story of Acts of the Apostles. Repentance, forgiveness, refreshing, the presence of the Lord—this is what Jesus offers us through his cross and resurrection. This is what the Holy Spirit longs to pour into the heart of every believer. This is what Peter, Paul, and all the apostles testified to as they spread out from Jerusalem to preach the good news.

God wants to refresh his people. He wants to lift from us the burden of our sins and fill us instead with the presence of Jesus. He wants to assure us that we are his beloved children and that he has nothing but good intentions for us. He wants to fill us with confidence and boldness to go out and preach the gospel just as the first apostles did. And yet, as the stories in Acts make clear, it's up to us whether we will receive these blessings or keep Jesus at a distance.

How can we embrace these "times of refreshing" from the Lord? If we look at the Book of Acts, we could agree with Peter that repentance is the key. And yet, a deeper look shows us that this repentance goes far beyond a simple apology to God. Throughout this book, we see that those who are closest to the Lord are the ones who have turned their lives over to Jesus and dedicated themselves to serving him completely. They are the "apostles" whose "acts" continue to encourage us today to give our hearts and our energies to the Lord.

It is our hope that this commentary on the Book of Acts will help you experience the same power of the Holy Spirit that the apostles knew. We believe that whenever God's people take time to ponder his word in Scripture, his Spirit moves in them. He reveals the love of Jesus. He convinces us of our forgiveness. He urges us to seek unity with one another. And he sends us out into the world as his witnesses. May we all become apostles right in our own homes, churches, and neighborhoods!

We want to thank everyone who has made this commentary possible, especially all the writers who contributed meditations. Some of the meditations appearing in this book were initially developed for *The Word Among Us* monthly publication, and we are grateful to these writers for granting us permission to reprint their work. We also want to thank Fr. Joseph Mindling, O.F.M. Cap., Patricia Mitchell, and Hallie Riedel for contributing the longer chapters, as well as Fr. Joseph Wimmer, O.S.A., for his help in reviewing the manuscript. May the Lord abundantly bless them all.

Leo Zanchettin
General Editor

Table of Contents

An Introduction to the Acts of the Apostles

By Fr. Joseph A. Mindling, O.F.M. Cap.

The Acts of the Apostles is a unique and colorful pane in that "rose window" of revelation which we call the New Testament. It is the only history of the earliest, formative period of the Christian community which was penned by a first-generation convert and managed to survive through tumultuous years of persecution, expansion, and change. Starting in Jerusalem with Jesus' ascension, its story line leads us through a series of episodes, covering about three decades and climaxing with the proclamation of the gospel in the capital of the Roman Empire.

Not long before this text first appeared around the year 85 A.D., the synoptic gospels and numerous pastoral letters had already been telling the world about Jesus of Nazareth. However, more and more time was separating second-generation Christians from the years of Jesus' public ministry and from the dramatic days of his crucifixion and resurrection. "Acts"—as this book is often called—was written to assure both them and all future believers that what had been happening during those intervening years of intense missionary activity was truly the divinely directed development of what Jesus had begun.

The Chronicles of Luke. Tradition tells us that the inspired author of the Acts of the Apostles was the same person who was responsible for the Gospel according to Luke. In fact, the two volumes were written to complement one another by highlighting important parallels between the Master and his successors. A very fruitful way to learn more about both books is to read them with a close eye to the way the episodes from the life of the early church depict the disciples following in Jesus' footsteps. Like their Master before them, they too were bearers of the good news, tireless teachers, miracle workers, defenders of the oppressed, dedicated to prayer, and, inevitably, victims of those who tried to block their role as agents of the Holy Spirit.

Luke could write knowledgeably about the community of believers of his day because he was an active participant in the history that he was chronicling. Referred to by his colleague Paul as the "beloved physician" (Colossians 4:14), this well-educated writer was among the most talented proclaimers of the Christian message in the apostolic era. And yet, as diligent and professional as Luke was in gathering the information he needed for this project, he was still able to compose his account in a popular style as engaging as that of a modern bestseller.

The title, "Acts of the Apostles," might lead us to expect a separate report on each of the Twelve whom Jesus had appointed as leaders in his church. In fact, all of them are mentioned in the first chapter, along with the account of the election of Matthias to replace Judas Iscariot. Surprisingly, though, most of the apostles are never mentioned again anywhere else in the book. Instead, Luke chose to focus primarily on two major figures—Peter and Paul—and two minor ones—Philip and Stephen—selecting episodes from their careers which were typical of those precedent-setting times.

To identify more clearly some of the truths and values Luke wanted to highlight, let's consider three important themes which recur in the stories he tells.

Good News and Personal Transformation. Acts frequently draws our attention to the topic of religious conversion. The first third of the book looks primarily at Peter's courageous leadership in Palestine, while the later chapters describe Paul's missionary trips that extended from

Damascus to Rome. Obviously, these eager evangelizers had to challenge their listeners to a change of heart: to renounce sin and to commit themselves in faith to Jesus. What may seem somewhat unexpected, though, is the way Luke emphasizes how both these men had to accept profound changes in their own thinking and actions in order to live up to so high a calling.

Perhaps because Peter was Jesus' hand-chosen "foundation rock," we might think of him only in terms of his role as a proclaimer of repentance and a new way of life for others. Of course, this was a responsibility he carried out heroically, even though he was denounced and imprisoned for doing so. However, it took a personal rooftop revelation and the persistent faith of a Roman army officer to convince Peter that accepting non-Jewish candidates for baptism had to be part of his regular job description as well. Faced with the unmistakable power of the Spirit at work in these events, Peter changed his mind and heart and publicly acknowledged that "God shows no partiality. Rather, in every nation whoever fears him and acts uprightly is acceptable to the Lord" (Acts 10:1-48).

Later, at what is often called the Council of Jerusalem, Luke shows Peter earnestly defending the very conviction which he had formerly resisted: Gentiles could become Christians without first adopting obsolete religious practices (Acts 15:1-21). Whatever once prevented Peter and other Jewish Christians from opening their hearts and their social horizons to "outsiders" from other races and religions, it was no match for the insistent presence of the Holy Spirit.

An equally famous conversion reported in this book got its dramatic jump-start on the main caravan route between Jerusalem and Damascus. As a radical rabbinical student, Paul of Tarsus did not realize that by hounding Jesus' followers, he was persecuting the Messiah himself. A flash of light brighter than the sun, a personal conversation with the Risen One, and three days of blindness reversed Paul's religious preconceptions rather abruptly. Luke considered this event such a crucial episode in the development of the church that he recounted it three separate times (Acts 9:3-9; 22:6-16; 26:12-18).

The challenge that Jesus laid out for Paul at that time serves as the gateway into the latter chapters of the book which report the conversion of countless others in response to his preaching. Born a Diaspora Pharisee and now a baptized Christian, Paul brought outstanding talents to his new assignment: his years of rabbinical training, his ability to interact with people of very diverse cultures, and his fearless fortitude. Yet Luke's lesson is clear. The Lord calls unlikely candidates to spread the good news, and evangelization must be an ongoing process in their own lives as well. In other words, to share the gospel effectively with others, we must let it go on changing us.

The Empowering Presence of the Holy Spirit. The Book of Acts reminds readers repeatedly that it is *divine providence* which guides and protects the spread of the faith. Frequent and explicit references to the activity of the Holy Spirit throughout the text are the most obvious affirmations of God's presence and direct role in the life of the church. In the very first chapter, right before the mission of the apostles begins, Jesus tells those gathered around him on the day of his ascension not to depart from Jerusalem but to "wait for the promise of the Father about which you have heard me speak; for John baptized with water, but in a few days you will be baptized with the Holy Spirit. . . . You will receive power when the Holy Spirit comes upon you, and you will be my witnesses in Jerusalem, throughout Judea and Samaria, and to the ends of the earth" (Acts 1:4-5,8).

These words make it clear from the outset that the descent of the Spirit on Mary and the apostles was not simply an isolated, dramatic moment; it was a pivotal event for the future life of the church. Its immediate effect was to provide the tools and the courage needed to continue to proclaim the paschal mystery. After nine days of nervous hiding, Peter and the other disciples were now able to confront an enormous and rather skeptical crowd. Transformed by the Spirit, they were able to speak in tongues or use their own language and still be understood by the international pilgrims gathered to celebrate the feast of Pentecost. "Those who accepted his message were baptized, and about three thousand persons were added that day" (Acts 2:41).

As Luke's account unfolds, the special presence of the Spirit continues to permeate the community with many other expressions of the power Jesus had promised. Sometimes this takes the form of an infusion of knowledge; sometimes it brings about decisive action. It is the Spirit who directs Philip to approach a royal official from Ethiopia, who instructs Peter to accept the invitation to teach at Caesarea, and who informs the prophet Agabus about an imminent famine. Perhaps the most often quoted recognition of inspired understanding is stated at the Council of Jerusalem: "It has seemed good to the Holy Spirit and to us to lay upon you no greater burden than these necessary things" (Acts 15:28; see also 8:29; 10:19; 11:28).

At other times, this supernatural guidance expresses itself in the discernment of God's word in the Scriptures, or in the choice of individual missionaries. In their ministry, the Spirit was not a force to be underestimated, as we see in the abrupt punishments of some who tried to work against it, such as Ananias and Sapphira, and the magicians Elymas and Simon (Acts 5:1-10; 8:18-24; 13:6-11). Those who read Acts and the Gospel of Luke attentively are reminded time and again that the interventions of the Spirit are as varied and as powerful as God's chosen ones need them to be.

The Great Cost of Faithful Perseverance. After centuries of successful expansion, the Christian community might be tempted to romanticize the "good old days" when the first wave of witnesses was still alive. Indeed, Luke reports instances of great spiritual idealism, such as daily prayer in common, pooling material possessions to eliminate economic inequality in the community, and heroic dedication to the spread of the faith in foreign lands. However, the Acts of the Apostles is a monument to the fact that in the face of fierce opposition, the spread of the faith was achieved only at the cost of relentless toil and repeated bloodshed. For communities who paid this price, the joy of winning new brothers and sisters to share their faith in Jesus was exhilarating, but Luke counterbalances any tendency to glamorize those early years with many sobering facts.

Civil violence and religious plots against the followers of Jesus thread their way through every major section of this book. At one point Luke quotes Paul as saying: "It is through many persecutions that we must enter the kingdom of God" (Acts 14:22). Paul and Peter both suffered unjust treatment in the courts and repeated imprisonment. The early chapters of Acts tell of great numbers forced to resettle in foreign cities because Christian families could no longer live safely in the Holy Land after the stoning of Stephen. Herod Agrippa had James, the first bishop of Jerusalem, beheaded.

Writing to the Corinthians, Paul had enumerated an impressive list of the tribulations he had endured during his many years as a missionary; he concluded by observing that "apart from these things, there is the daily pressure upon me of my anxiety for all the churches" (2 Corinthians 11:28). In addition to recording opposition the Christian community faced from outside its ranks, Acts helps us to imagine what some internal sources of these concerns might have been:

- Widows of Greek-speaking Christians complaining that they were not receiving a fair amount of the alms donated for their support (6:1);

- Paul and Barnabas unable to resolve their differences over John Mark and no longer working together as a missionary team (15:36-40);

- Eutychus falling out a window to his death because Paul's lengthy preaching at an evening prayer service had put him to sleep (20:7-12);

- Leading Christians in Jerusalem remaining preoccupied with what the Jewish community thought about their faithfulness to Mosaic law (21:15-26).

Nevertheless, these very human problems may be among the most appealing elements in this book. If we let them remind us of our own struggles today to live up to the ideals Jesus has held out to us, surely we can be encouraged and inspired by many other elements in this account as well.

St. Paul assures us that "all Scripture is inspired by God and is useful for teaching, for refutation, for correction, and for training in righteousness" (2 Timothy 3:16). We can harvest these benefits if we prayerfully immerse ourselves in Luke's memoirs. What he and the Holy Spirit have captured in the Acts of the Apostles are but the first chapters of a history that continues to unfold in our own experience as Christians. Yes, Acts is also about us.

The Apostles on a First-Century Stage

A Historical Backdrop to the Book of Acts

By Patricia Mitchell

At its most basic level, the Acts of the Apostles is a historical account of how the apostles spread the gospel and built the church. The stories Luke tells in Acts happened a long time ago—not in some vacuum, but in a specific time and place which in many ways is unfamiliar to twenty-first-century Christians. Like any other time in history, first-century Palestine was filled with competing political interests, philosophies, and religions, all of which had a bearing on the apostles' mission. Let's try to "fill in the gaps" left by St. Luke in his relatively short Book of Acts by setting the story in a historical context.

The Political Environment. The Book of Acts opens shortly after Jesus' death and resurrection, around 30 A.D. The political situation of that time could best be described as tense. Palestine had been under Roman rule for more than sixty years, beginning in 37 B.C., when the Romans installed Herod as king. Although he was himself Jewish, Herod alienated his people by his brutality and greed. When Herod died in 4 B.C., his sons and then his grandson, Herod Agrippa, succeeded him. Hatred against Roman rule persisted throughout this period, occasionally erupting in violence.

Although Acts reads like a fast-paced adventure story, the events in the book actually take place over a span of thirty years. During that time, a series of Roman procurators governed Palestine, including two who are named in Acts: Felix (Acts 23:26), who took office in 52 A.D., and Porcius Festus (24:27), who assumed his post in 60 A.D. The Book of

Acts ends with Paul living under house arrest in Rome, without any major change in the political situation. But, only several years later, Jewish sentiment against the Romans finally exploded in a show of force, with revolutionaries seizing the Roman citadel in Jerusalem.

This was a defining moment for the Jews, one that Jesus foretold in the gospels (Matthew 24; Mark 13; Luke 21). When the Romans retaliated in 70 A.D., they marched on Jerusalem, burning the temple in the process. Before it was completely engulfed in flames, the Roman general Titus desecrated the most sacred area of the temple, the Holy of Holies. The horrible "desolating abomination" (Daniel 11:31) so feared by the Jews finally came to pass.

The Temple. It can be difficult for us today to imagine the significance of the temple to first-century Jews. A traveler approaching the holy city would have been stunned by the beauty of the temple, an imposing structure that sat atop a hill and could be seen for miles away. Under Herod, the temple had been restored and the temple grounds enlarged. Even Gentiles were allowed to enter its outer court. On sabbaths and religious festivals, the high priest—who was the head of the Sanhedrin—conducted services with the other chief priests in the temple.

A pilgrim entering Jerusalem would gravitate first to the temple area, the center of life for the Jewish community. Sacrifices were offered daily, and thousands of pilgrims converged on the city for the great feasts of Passover, Pentecost, and Tabernacles. On that Pentecost when the Holy Spirit descended on the apostles, it would have been natural that in Jerusalem, there were Jews "from every nation under heaven" (Acts 2:5). These were the pilgrims who had come to the holy city for the feast, and on that day, they heard the apostles speaking to them in their own language.

Luke tells us that not long after Pentecost, when Peter and John were on their way to the temple to pray, they healed a lame man (Acts 3:1-10). Like any devout Jew in Jerusalem at the time, they would have gone to the temple even for private prayer. Peter subsequently preached to a crowd of Jews who had also gone to the temple to pray. Because the priests were from Sadducean families, they would have been especially annoyed that Peter and John were "proclaiming in Jesus the resurrection from the dead" (4:2). Despite the efforts of the priests and elders to prevent the apostles from preaching, it was clear that they would continue to do so—under the very noses of the priests in the temple area (5:12,42).

The Religious Environment. We might be inclined to think that the basic tenets of first-century Judaism were fixed in stone. This was true to some extent, but there were still plenty of areas open to discussion and disagreement. Members of a variety of religious groups or movements within Judaism were quite passionate in defending their convictions— often against one another. These groups included the Pharisees, the Sadducees, the Zealots, and the celibate community known as the Essenes. Each group had a different "take" on what they saw as the requirements of Judaism and the extent of Jewish interaction permissible with the world. Each would have reacted slightly differently to the message of the apostles.

Probably the most offensive idea expounded by the apostles was that the Gentiles were also included in the new covenant of God. The concept of "uncleanness," which included consorting with Gentiles, was so ingrained in the Jewish mind that even Peter found it difficult to accept that God was calling nothing unclean (Acts 10:14-16). Another difficult concept would have been the apostles' teaching of the resurrection of Jesus. This would have especially upset the chief priests and many of the Sanhedrin who, as Sadducees, discounted talk of the resurrection as a myth that could not be found in the Law of Moses (Matthew 22:23-33; Acts 5:17-18; 23:6-8).

Despite these differences in outlook, however, Jews were remarkably united in their fundamental views about God and the Law. The confession, "Hear, O Israel, the LORD our God is one LORD," was the foundation of their prayer and belief. The Torah—the first five books of the Old Testament that comprise the Mosaic law—possessed unquestionable authority and was revered as the word of God. All Jews were convinced about the necessity of following the Law, even if there were varying interpretations of how rigorously it should be followed. All Jews, too, believed in a coming salvation, although some thought that a long-awaited messiah would liberate his people while others believed this would happen through a miraculous deed of God. False messiahs were common enough—two are even mentioned in Acts (5:36-37).

The Diaspora. Surprisingly enough, at the time Acts was written, more Jews lived outside of Palestine than within the borders of their homeland. Jews were forced to leave Palestine beginning in 587 B.C. with the Babylonian exile, a tragedy known as the Diaspora. Over the centuries, many Jews were forcibly removed as prisoners of various wars. Oppressive taxes caused others to leave, as did a lack of economic opportunities.

Over time, synagogues became the glue that held the exiled Jewish communities together, keeping its beliefs and way of life intact in a foreign environment. In every area where there was a Jewish population, there would have been a synagogue—a place to hold worship services, to study the Law, and to teach the children the traditions of their ancestors. Even outside their homeland, the Romans had granted special concessions to the Jews, such as freedom from military service and the right to worship in their synagogues.

A worship service in a synagogue consisted of common, recited prayer, Scripture reading, and instruction. Prayer was offered at the same intervals as in the Jerusalem temple, and always included the confession that there is only one true God. Any adult male member of the community was permitted to read Scripture or preach. When Paul arrived in a new city on his missionary journeys, he went first to the synagogue to preach about Jesus (Acts 13:14; 14:1; 17:1-2; 18:4; 19:8). Sometimes, through his exposition of the prophecies in the Old Testament, he was able to convince some of the members of the congregation that Jesus was the fulfillment of the Law and the true Messiah. At other times, he was forced to leave the synagogue and preach to the Gentiles, often in public places (19:9).

Although Jews living outside Palestine were periodically subject to ridicule and even violence, their belief in one God and their adherence to a strict ethical code did at times attract the attention of Gentiles. Those who wanted to hear about the Law often became "God-fearers." They did not fully convert and submit to circumcision, but they did confess belief in the one God and observed the sabbath and dietary rules. Cornelius (Acts 10:22) and Lydia (16:14) were probably both "God-fearers" before their conversion to Christianity.

Cultural Influences. As much as they needed to remain a separate and distinct community, the Jews of the Diaspora were influenced by the culture that surrounded them. They were especially attracted to the Greeks' intellectual skills, which helped them justify their own faith. Eventually many knew no other language than Greek. Sometimes they could obtain Roman citizenship. Paul, for instance, was a Diaspora Jew from Tarsus who had Roman citizenship and could speak both Hebrew and Greek. Paul's knowledge of Greek philosophy was a great aid to him as he preached the gospel, especially in Athens, where he spoke with Epicurean and Stoic philosophers and quoted some of their sayings (Acts 17:28) to prove the reality of God and the hope of salvation in Christ.

In contrast to the unity of belief and action of Judaism, the prevailing religions in the Roman Empire were a mix of philosophy and superstition. A host of Greek and Roman gods was venerated, and beautiful shrines were dedicated in their honor. Sorcery and magic were commonly practiced. In time, a cult of the emperor developed, and Romans were required to pay reverence to whoever occupied the throne at the time—although this did not prevent them from practicing their own religion as well. Jews were exempted from these requirements, but as

Christianity separated from Judaism, Christians were executed for refusing to participate in this mandatory ritual.

Epicurean thinking, one of the popular philosophies of the day, denied an afterlife and so emphasized a well-balanced, pleasant life coupled with a kind of withdrawal from the world. The Stoics saw the world as filled with the divine presence of a god who governs the universe and calls on men and women to live in harmony with the natural laws and to fulfill the tasks assigned to them. These beliefs became fertile ground for acceptance of Christianity.

The Word in the World. God chose a particular time and place in history to send his Son to redeem his people, and Scripture writers tell the story of salvation within that context. When we learn more about the historical backdrop of the Book of Acts, and of the New Testament in general, the word of God can become more than ink on a page—it can come to life. As you use this devotional commentary, may the stories of the first apostles become vivid reminders of God's loving interventions in the world—both then and now.

A Spiritual Obstacle Course

Who Said Building the Church Should Be Easy?

By Hallie Riedel

I magine that you've been asked to form a new organization. Now, suppose that the immediate future holds the following: astronomic growth, rejection by your parent organization, being labeled by the government as illegal, persecution that leads to a dispersal of your members, no established organization or structure, a centuries-old feud between two rival ethnic groups, and almost continual harassment of your leaders. Who would even want to take on a task fraught with such hurdles? Yet this is a sampling of the challenges faced by the first Christians in the Book of Acts. How did these early believers cope?

Let's start at the beginning. Once Jesus had ascended to heaven (Acts 1:6-11), the apostles awaited the coming of the Holy Spirit. But even before the Spirit came, they faced their first major challenge: Who should replace Judas? Their answer—praying and then drawing lots—may seem superstitious, but it demonstrated an early stage of experimentation in prayerfully listening to the Holy Spirit.

Having chosen Matthias, the apostles were ready for Pentecost. Filled with the power of the Spirit, they boldly proclaimed the glory of God and as a result, three thousand Jewish worshipers were converted that day. And the numbers just kept growing. In a very short time, this group of believers had grown from a handful to a throng: "Day by day the Lord added to their number those who were being saved" (Acts 2:47).

Luke tells us that the fledgling church was faithful to "the apostles' teaching and fellowship, to the breaking of bread and the prayers" (Acts 2:42). But living in common as they had in the earliest days (1:13) eventually became impractical for such a large group, so they made a point of pooling their resources instead and distributing them according to need (4:32).

Reversal of Fortune and Bitter Animosity. For a while, things were looking up for the infant church: Being Jews, church members enjoyed official acceptance by the Roman government as an "authorized religion." They continued to worship in the temple, and "the people held them in high honor" (Acts 5:13). But as the apostles and leaders appeared more frequently before the Sanhedrin and were subjected to increasing interrogations and floggings, a split from Judaism seemed unavoidable. After the death of Stephen, the gathering storm clouds broke open and unleashed a bitter persecution. No longer accepted or tolerated by the Jews, and now considered an illegal sect by the Romans, the believers scattered throughout Judea and Samaria.

Such a reversal of fortune would have meant the end for any other organization. But the Holy Spirit was in charge of this group, and Jesus himself, the Son of God, had commanded his followers to preach to all nations, beginning in Jerusalem (Luke 24:47; Acts 1:8). No one would have chosen persecution, but it was through persecution that the tight-knit community scattered and "went from place to place proclaiming the word" (8:4). Believers fled to Samaria, Gaza, Joppa, Lydda, and even faraway Antioch. Everywhere they went, they brought the presence and the power of the Holy Spirit with them. Hearts were changed, demons were cast out, the sick were healed, and Jesus was proclaimed as Messiah and Lord.

But it still wasn't enough. God had more in store for these early disciples than just sending them to a few outposts in the Near East. In two more surprising series of events, one of the church's principal persecutors, Saul of Tarsus, was converted (Acts 9:1-19), and Peter received an unusual vision that led to the baptism of an entire household of Gentiles (10:1-48). It looked as if the church would only continue to win out over its enemies and expand far beyond the disciples' expectations.

New Opportunities, New Challenges. What would seem to have been an encouraging event—acceptance of Christ by Gentiles and subsequent missionary trips into pagan territory—became a challenge that threatened to pull the new church apart. Peter's vision, in which God told him not to consider unclean what God had declared clean, set the stage for a radical new idea: preaching to non-Jews about Jesus the Messiah. When put in a situation which challenged long-standing animosities against the Gentiles, Peter felt he was being led by the Spirit to live out the teachings of Jesus, who healed a centurion's servant (Luke 7:1-10) and said "you will know them by their fruits" (Matthew 7:16). So, when the Holy Spirit came down on Cornelius and his household, Peter simply couldn't refuse them the water of baptism. The "fruit" of the Spirit was too clear.

But the animosity between Jews and Gentiles was not so easily overcome. So ancient an enmity needed a deeper working of the Holy Spirit in many more people before it could be healed. As Paul began his first missionary journey with Barnabas, he received such harsh treatment at the hands of some Jews that he turned away from the synagogue and went to the Gentiles instead (Acts 13:46). Later, after these two returned to their home at Antioch, a controversy erupted when some believers from Judea arrived and told the gentile Christians that they had to follow the Mosaic law to be saved. The question raged: Did the gift of salvation depend upon obedience to the Mosaic law, or did it come solely by grace?

What could the elders of the church do in the face of so deep-seated a conflict? This was uncharted territory. What they were trying to do in bringing Jews and Gentiles together as equals was completely revolutionary. When the elders met in Jerusalem, Peter recounted what the Spirit had taught him through his encounter with Cornelius. Then James recalled a prophecy from Scripture that all nations were meant to turn to the Lord. Clearly, the believers could not allow animosities, no matter how strong, to interfere with the way Jesus had chosen to build his church. This was God's doing. So, they sent a letter to all the believers saying, "It has seemed good *to the Holy Spirit* and to us to impose on you no further burden than these essentials" (Acts 15:28, emphasis added). Only a few specific pagan practices, they said, should be avoided.

Spirit, Structure, or Both? Thus the church opened itself up to countless new believers, and the gospel was free to spread "to the ends of the earth," as Jesus had promised it would (Acts 1:8). But who could map out such a massive missionary effort? Who would determine where to go? It is in this "obstacle" that we see dramatic interventions of the Holy Spirit. The Spirit specifically told Paul not to preach in Asia but beckoned him to Macedonia instead (16:6-10). Later, on his way to Jerusalem, Paul promised he would return to Ephesus only if the Spirit willed (18:21), because he understood that it was the Spirit who had impelled him to the holy city (20:22-23). Time and time again, we see that what no human could have orchestrated came to pass through the power of the Holy Spirit: Jesus Christ was being proclaimed to the ends of the earth!

As the gospel continued to spread throughout the world, believers faced questions of a more intricate matter. It may be difficult for us today to imagine a church with no set Eucharistic liturgy, formula for baptisms, or guidelines for communal prayer. The church had to balance openness to the movement of the Holy Spirit with the need to remain faithful to Jesus' teaching in the face of "inspired" heresies. At first, the apostles themselves intervened, verifying the validity of conversions and praying for believers to receive the Holy Spirit (Acts 8:14-17). But later, as in the case of the gentile question, they conferred together and sent their decisions to remote areas by letter with missionaries (15:22-23).

Believers grappled with issues of formal worship as well. Early liturgical writings such as the Didache show remarkable similarity to Jewish forms of worship, adapting traditionally Jewish prayers to the new Eucharistic celebration. Persecution forced the church to make the transition from communal worship at the temple or synagogues to meeting in private homes or just outside the town limits (Acts 16:13). These transitions, made necessary by circumstances, were actually led by the Holy Spirit to bring the church to maturity in Christ.

Leaders in Chains. From the beginning, the church faced the perplexing dilemma of having its leaders imprisoned, punished, and killed by religious and secular authorities. One would think that such a situation would demoralize the church, perhaps even break it apart. But just the opposite happened. Early threats and floggings from the Sanhedrin only strengthened the resolve of these early Christians to obey God, and the Lord himself confirmed that they were on the right track (4:23-31). On some occasions, the apostles were even miraculously delivered from certain death as yet another sign that God was indeed with them (5:18-21; 12:6-11; 16:25-34).

The deaths of the first martyrs unleashed the Spirit's power to build the church anew. The blood of Stephen (Acts 7:55-60) and James (12:2) brought about many conversions, most obviously Paul, who had approved of Stephen's stoning. Implicitly, Paul's impending death while imprisoned in Rome (28:11-15) also strengthened the church and the spread of the gospel. These executions, terrible as they were, allowed the Holy Spirit to demonstrate that Jesus truly did found the church, and that only he—not forceful or popular leaders—could keep it together.

Course Completed? As we look at the story of the early church's "obstacle course," we can make a few conclusions:

- The Holy Spirit is always with the church, leading and guiding it.

- Even in the worst of circumstances, God can bring great blessing, encouragement, and even deliverance.

• Sometimes it is necessary for believers to confront obstacles in order to enter more fully into the life Jesus intends them to have.

While the early church faced issues and problems that would seem quite foreign to us, the same Holy Spirit is at work today, seeking to bring about the very same goal: to make all the people of God more like Jesus the Savior.

The Time Has Come

ACTS
1

Acts 1:1-14

[1] In the first book, O Theophilus, I have dealt with all that Jesus began to do and teach, [2] until the day when he was taken up, after he had given commandment through the Holy Spirit to the apostles whom he had chosen. [3] To them he presented himself alive after his passion by many proofs, appearing to them during forty days, and speaking of the kingdom of God. [4] And while staying with them he charged them not to depart from Jerusalem, but to wait for the promise of the Father, which, he said, "you heard from me, [5] for John baptized with water, but before many days you shall be baptized with the Holy Spirit."

[6] So when they had come together, they asked him, "Lord, will you at this time restore the kingdom to Israel?" [7] He said to them, "It is not for you to know times or seasons which the Father has fixed by his own authority. [8] But you shall receive power when the Holy Spirit has come upon you; and you shall be my witnesses in Jerusalem and in all Judea and Samaria and to the end of the earth."

[9] And when he had said this, as they were looking on, he was lifted up, and a cloud took him out of their sight. [10] And while they were gazing into heaven as he went, behold, two men stood by them in white robes, [11] and said, "Men of Galilee, why do you stand looking into heaven? This Jesus, who was taken up from you into heaven, will come in the same way as you saw him go into heaven."

[12] Then they returned to Jerusalem from the mount called Olivet, which is near Jerusalem, a sabbath day's journey away; [13] and when they had entered, they went up to the upper room, where they were staying, Peter and John and James and Andrew, Philip and Thomas, Bartholomew and Matthew, James the son of Alphaeus and Simon the Zealot and Judas the son of James. [14] All these with one accord devoted themselves to prayer, together with the women and Mary the mother of Jesus, and with his brothers. ☞

Imagine what was going through the disciples' minds as they saw Jesus ascend to heaven. The past few weeks consisted of dizzying changes, and it seemed that more were yet to come. Their world was turned upside down when they saw Jesus arrested and put to death. Their hearts must have been wounded almost beyond repair at the betrayal and injustice they saw heaped upon him. Then came the excitement, even shock, of seeing him risen from the dead, still bearing the marks of the cross!

After the ups and downs of the preceding weeks, Jesus now promised them something new, something comforting: "You shall receive power when the Holy Spirit has come upon you; and you shall be my witnesses . . . to the ends of the earth" (Acts 1:8). These words must have been very encouraging indeed! They would not be left alone, but would receive the strength and guidance of God in their very hearts.

The same promises apply today. Jesus is still enthroned in heaven with the Father, and his promise to return to us still holds true (Acts 1:11). On that day, God "will wipe away every tear from their eyes, and death shall be no more, neither shall there be mourning nor crying nor pain any more" (Revelation 21:4). What's more, Jesus has sent the Holy Spirit to teach us, empower us, and keep us united with Jesus until the final day. These are the promises we celebrate.

While the apostles waited for the Spirit to come, they spent their days in prayer (Acts 1:12-14). As we await Jesus' glorious return, let us imitate them by praying every day for more of the Spirit. God's love is more abundant than we have yet known. Who can tell what grace awaits us as we grow closer to the Spirit? Let us never think we have enough of the Spirit, but let us say always, "Fill us, Lord!"

"Jesus, we rejoice with heaven as we celebrate your ascension. You are the risen King, the Lion of the Tribe of Judah! May all creation praise you, today and forever!"

Acts 1:15-26

[15] In those days Peter stood up among the brethren (the company of persons was in all about a hundred and twenty), and said,
[16] "Brethren, the scripture had to be fulfilled, which the Holy Spirit spoke beforehand by the mouth of David, concerning Judas who was guide to those who arrested Jesus. [17] For he was numbered among us, and was allotted his share in this ministry. [18] (Now this man bought a field with the reward of his wickedness; and falling headlong he burst open in the middle and all his bowels gushed out. [19] And it became known to all the inhabitants of Jerusalem, so that the field was called in their language Akeldama, that is, Field of Blood.)
[20] For it is written in the book of Psalms, 'Let his habitation become desolate, and let there be no one to live in it'; and 'His office let another take.' [21] So one of the men who have accompanied us during all the time that the Lord Jesus went in and out among us, [22] beginning from the baptism of John until the day when he was taken up from us—one of these men must become with us a witness to his resurrection." [23] And they put forward two, Joseph called Barsabbas, who was surnamed Justus, and Matthias.
[24] And they prayed and said, "Lord, who knowest the hearts of all men, show which one of these two thou hast chosen [25] to take the place in this ministry and apostleship from which Judas turned aside, to go to his own place." [26] And they cast lots for them, and the lot fell on Matthias; and he was enrolled with the eleven apostles.

Matthias was chosen by God to replace Judas Iscariot as the twelfth apostle. What was it about Matthias that caused the lot to fall to him? Was he chosen because he was perfect and sinless? No. The Father saw something in Matthias that was far more important—a heart that was changed by experiencing the risen Christ.

It is the transforming power of the death and resurrection of Jesus, and nothing else, that makes anyone a suitable candidate for apostleship. It is believing that Jesus is Lord and Savior and asking him to live inside of us that enables all of us to be his disciples. Remember: Jesus called ordinary people—who had their own share of faults and sinful tendencies—to be his followers. He wanted to make sure that everyone knew that the power that they demonstrated came from him and not from their own natural resources.

To understand this truth, let's take a look at Judas—whom Matthias replaced—and Peter. Both men failed Jesus in his darkest hour. Judas betrayed him, and Peter denied ever knowing him. For both men, these sins were overwhelming, but they responded in completely different ways. Judas could neither forgive himself nor accept forgiveness, and so he was lost. Peter, however, wept tears of repentance, and so he was saved. This moment was critical in Peter's transformation into an apostle. He did not let his failure get in the way of his love for Jesus.

More than anything else, the world is in desperate need of apostles who will carry on the call of the first Twelve to bear witness to the resurrection of Jesus. Will you accept his call? Don't believe for a minute that you are not pure enough or holy enough. Jesus knows our hearts. All he asks is that we confess our sins, turn to him, receive his Spirit, and witness by the way we live that Jesus Christ is Lord. Matthias was not perfect, and Peter was not perfect. But this did not deter them from their call. They accepted the grace of Jesus and were changed and formed into his servants.

"Thank you, Jesus, for the transforming power of your mercy, which turned twelve ordinary men into apostles. Thank you that this same power can transform me as well. Release your Holy Spirit in me today so that my life may be a living testimony to your resurrection."

The Story of Pentecost

ACTS
2

Acts 2:1-13

[1] When the day of Pentecost had come, they were all together in one place. [2] And suddenly a sound came from heaven like the rush of a mighty wind, and it filled all the house where they were sitting. [3] And there appeared to them tongues as of fire, distributed and resting on each one of them. [4] And they were all filled with the Holy Spirit and began to speak in other tongues, as the Spirit gave them utterance. [5] Now there were dwelling in Jerusalem Jews, devout men from every nation under heaven. [6] And at this sound the multitude came together, and they were bewildered, because each one heard them speaking in his own language. [7] And they were amazed and wondered, saying, "Are not all these who are speaking Galileans? [8] And how is it that we hear, each of us in his own native language? [9] Parthians and Medes and Elamites and residents of Mesopotamia, Judea and Cappadocia, Pontus and Asia, [10] Phrygia and Pamphylia, Egypt and the parts of Libya belonging to Cyrene, and visitors from Rome, both Jews and proselytes, [11] Cretans and Arabians, we hear them telling in our own tongues the mighty works of God." [12] And all were amazed and perplexed, saying to one another, "What does this mean?" [13] But others mocking said, "They are filled with new wine."

From a homily by St. Leo the Great (c. 400-461):

"If I do not go," Jesus told his apostles, "the Advocate will not come to you. But if I go away, then I will send him to you" (John 16:7). "Do not leave Jerusalem, but wait there for the gift my Father promised, the gift of which I told you. John baptized with water, but in a few days' time you will be baptized with the Holy Spirit" (Acts 1:4-5).

These were the Lord's parting words to his disciples. . . . Not that the Spirit would only begin to work among men after Jesus had returned to the Father; he had been at work in the world since the dawn of creation. God's people were not to experience a hitherto unknown indwelling of the Holy Spirit, but those who already belonged to him would know a more abundant outpouring, an increase rather than a first reception of his gifts.

Pentecost is the culmination of the work of our salvation, that mighty plan of God's mercy which originated long ago when the Lord first began to form a people for himself. How many mysterious signs can be discovered in this feast which link the old dispensation with the new, teaching us that the Law of Moses was the herald of the grace of Christ, in which it was to find its fulfillment!

Fifty days after the sacrifice of the lamb marking the deliverance of the Hebrews from the Egyptians, the Law was given to the people of Israel on Sinai; and fifty days from the resurrection of Christ after his immolation as the true Lamb of God, the Holy Spirit came down upon the new Israel, the people who put their faith in Jesus. The same Holy Spirit was the author of both Old and New Testaments; the foundations of the gospel were laid with the establishment of the old covenant.

The perennial message of the gospel is that the Lord has saved his people. He has conquered sin and death, and given us new life as God's adopted sons. And because we are sons, God has sent the Spirit of his Son into our hearts, crying, "Abba, Father!" (Galatians 4:6). Now where the Spirit of the Lord is, there is freedom (2 Corinthians 3:17). We are no longer slaves, but free men. It belongs to the dignity of free men to play some part in their own salvation; our task is to elude the enemy's clutches by constantly turning in repentance to our Redeemer and proclaiming that Jesus is Lord.

Acts 2:14-21

[14] But Peter, standing with the eleven, lifted up his voice and addressed them, "Men of Judea and all who dwell in Jerusalem, let this be known to you, and give ear to my words. [15] For these men are not drunk, as you suppose, since it is only the third hour of the day; [16] but this is what was spoken by the prophet Joel: [17] 'And in the last days it shall be, God declares, that I will pour out my Spirit upon all flesh, and your sons and your daughters shall prophesy, and your young men shall see visions, and your old men shall dream dreams; [18] yea, and on my menservants and my maidservants in those days I will pour out my Spirit; and they shall prophesy. [19] And I will show wonders in the heaven above and signs on the earth beneath, blood, and fire, and vapor of smoke; [20] the sun shall be turned into darkness and the moon into blood, before the day of the Lord comes, the great and manifest day. [21] And it shall be that whoever calls on the name of the Lord shall be saved.' " 〽

How surprised the people must have been to hear what Peter was saying! In the midst of what seemed like holy chaos, he reminded the crowd that they were seeing the fulfillment of prophecy from their own beloved Hebrew Scripture. The promises were coming true. God was inaugurating a new era in which his people come to an intimate relationship with him—to the point that they are dreaming prophetic dreams and seeing visions from heaven.

Can you imagine the wonder that filled the people's minds as they heard the good news preached in their own language by uneducated Galileans? For those with open hearts, there must have been an interior leap of joy. The time of waiting had ended. Now was the time of fulfillment.

Reading a passage like this one can bring great joy to our hearts as well. All the blessings promised by the prophets are now ours. They were meant for no other purpose but to fill us with God's absolute infinite love so that we would be able to bring that love into the world. God is in us! He is for us! Nothing can prevail against us!

While it may seem as though the darkness in the world is increasing, we can be confident that God is pouring out his blessing and love even more abundantly. God is using even what may seem to be the most impossible of circumstances to draw us to himself and convince us of his providence. At times, it may feel as if the sun is being darkened and the moon is turning to blood, but anyone who rests in Christ remains secure.

Let us not shrink back in times of darkness but ask the Spirit to give us eyes to see what he is doing. Let us ask the Spirit for the confidence that Peter and all the others displayed on Pentecost Sunday. Let's allow Jesus into our hearts and know that God is completely trustworthy. As we do, we will see the promises Peter proclaimed come alive in us.

"Holy Spirit, thank you for this age of blessing in the church. Thank you for all the ways you are fanning into flame a deeper love for God the Father in my heart. Give me the confidence to live each day with my head held high because of your love. Lord, I want nothing less than more of you."

Acts 2:22-35

[22] "Men of Israel, hear these words: Jesus of Nazareth, a man attested to you by God with mighty works and wonders and signs which God did through him in your midst, as you yourselves know— [23] this Jesus, delivered up according to the definite plan and foreknowledge of God, you crucified and killed by the hands of lawless men. [24] But God raised him up, having loosed the pangs of death, because it was not possible for him to be held by it. [25] For David says concerning him, 'I saw the Lord always before me, for he is at my right hand that I may not be shaken; [26] therefore my heart was glad, and my tongue rejoiced; moreover my flesh will dwell in hope. [27] For thou wilt not abandon my soul to Hades, nor let thy Holy One see corruption. [28] Thou hast made known to me the ways of life; thou wilt make me full of gladness with thy presence.'

[29] "Brethren, I may say to you confidently of the patriarch David that he both died and was buried, and his tomb is with us to this day.
[30] Being therefore a prophet, and knowing that God had sworn with an oath to him that he would set one of his descendants upon his throne, [31] he foresaw and spoke of the resurrection of the Christ, that he was not abandoned to Hades, nor did his flesh see corruption.
[32] This Jesus God raised up, and of that we all are witnesses. [33] Being therefore exalted at the right hand of God, and having received from the Father the promise of the Holy Spirit, he has poured out this which you see and hear. [34] For David did not ascend into the heavens; but he himself says, 'The Lord said to my Lord, Sit at my right hand, [35] till I make thy enemies a stool for thy feet.' "

At the heart of the declaration of the good news of God in the early church was the Jesus *kerygma* (from the Greek word for "proclaim"), that is, the proclamation of the name, works, death, and resurrection of Jesus. The gospel centered around what God had done in Jesus, from his incarnation through his resurrection. The message of hope to a despairing world was that God had brought salvation to all people through his Son. Thus, the early church centered its teaching on Jesus—on his name, works, death, and resurrection.

Followers of Jesus came very early to understand that he had died and risen to new life in order that all people might find life in him. Peter, when he spoke to those gathered in Jerusalem on Pentecost (Acts 2:1,14), was living in the faith of the resurrection by the power of the Spirit dwelling in him. Through faith in the risen Lord, Peter came to experience in his own life the truth that Jesus' death and resurrection brought all those who believe from death to life.

Before Pentecost, a fearful Peter lacked confidence and conviction in what he now knew to be true. He was impetuous, boastful, and immature in his understanding of divine realities. After Pentecost, Peter was a transformed person. He became a fearless, confident disciple who boldly proclaimed the central place that Jesus has in the plan of salvation. He was alive with God's Spirit.

And so the heart of Peter's message focused on "Jesus of Nazareth," a man affirmed "by God with deeds of power, wonders and signs," a man whom, though crucified, God raised up and exalted. Now seated "at the right hand of God," he is "both Lord and Messiah!" (Acts 2:22-24,32-33,36). Peter experienced what he proclaimed—faith in Jesus risen and glorified. The victory at Calvary was his victory; the resurrection life was his life.

Like Peter, we are meant to share in the life of the risen Lord, through the Holy Spirit who dwells in us. And like Peter and all faithful Christians throughout the ages, God would have us experience so profoundly the truth of Jesus risen and alive that we would joyfully and fearlessly proclaim his name, works, death, and saving resurrection to all we meet.

Acts 2:36-41

[36] "Let all the house of Israel therefore know assuredly that God has made him both Lord and Christ, this Jesus whom you crucified." [37] Now when they heard this they were cut to the heart, and said to Peter and the rest of the apostles, "Brethren, what shall we do?" [38] And Peter said to them, "Repent, and be baptized every one of you in the name of Jesus Christ for the forgiveness of your sins; and you shall receive the gift of the Holy Spirit. [39] For the promise is to you and to your children and to all that are far off, every one whom the Lord our God calls to him." [40] And he testified with many other words and exhorted them, saying, "Save yourselves from this crooked generation." [41] So those who received his word were baptized, and there were added that day about three thousand souls.

How generous is our God! He *wants* to save us. He *wants* to fill us with divine life! It's not as if we have to convince him. *He* has called *us* to new life in him. The people listening to Peter were "cut to the heart" because they realized that their thinking and their lifestyles fell short of full communion with God (Acts 2:37). After turning away from their sins, they were baptized into new life through the Holy Spirit.

The gift of repentance is a grace-filled step in the process of change and transformation. God has many gifts and blessings in store for those who turn away from sin and seek to live a new life. He provides forgiveness, the gift of the Holy Spirit and, through Jesus, the fulfillment of all his promises. We need only make the decision to turn our hearts and lives over to God and ask him to free us from every sin that separates us from him.

On the cross, Jesus took upon himself the burden of all our sins, empowering us to walk in the dignity that comes from being God's children. In response to our repentance and faith, he gives us the Holy Spirit, who seeks to convict us of sin, assure us of Jesus' redemptive work, and empower us to live a new life. The Holy Spirit is always with us, convincing us that as we enter more deeply into our new lives as children of God, we can receive the fullness of his promises.

Today, let us be "cut to the heart," deeply desirous of the gift of repentance. God so wants to forgive us and bring us into his kingdom. When we repent, he does a tremendous work in us, offering us a new and different way of life, rich in his blessings. Are you experiencing freedom from sin? Do you know the gifts of the Holy Spirit such as peace, patience, kindness, and love? If you do not see the fullness of God's power at work in your life, ask him to lead you to a deeper repentance and into the fullness of his Spirit. Our God longs to provide us with all that we need to live in faith and grace each day.

"Father, thank you for your faithfulness and your wondrous gifts. I come to you in repentance, seeking to live my life in you. Help me to experience total newness in your Spirit."

Acts 2:42-47

[42] And they devoted themselves to the apostles' teaching and fellowship, to the breaking of bread and the prayers.
[43] And fear came upon every soul; and many wonders and signs were done through the apostles. [44] And all who believed were together and had all things in common; [45] and they sold their possessions and goods and distributed them to all, as any had need. [46] And day by day, attending the temple together and breaking bread in their homes, they partook of food with glad and generous hearts, [47] praising God and having favor with all the people. And the Lord added to their number day by day those who were being saved. ⏣

Our heavenly Father has given us a great gift: prayer. Think about the privilege we have of speaking freely with our Father any time we want. When we are rejoicing, when we are sad, when we are confused, when we need wisdom—God loves to hear us speak to him. The psalms poignantly illustrate this truth, for they are a rich treasury of prayers for every situation we may face.

Just before he ascended to heaven, Jesus told his disciples to wait in Jerusalem for the outpouring of the Holy Spirit. As they waited, they prayed together, and their times of prayer must have comforted them and fueled their expectations. We can imagine the hours they spent together, recalling all that Jesus had said and done while he was with them.

Ten days later, when the Holy Spirit came, they understood that a new way had been opened up for them to hear God and be filled with his life. They also experienced the Spirit leading them to pray (Acts 2:4). Prayer brought them into a deeper intimacy with Jesus than they had known before and filled them with the desires of the Father's heart. As a consequence, they found themselves wanting to be together to worship him (2:42).

God is delighted when we come to him with thanksgiving and praise. He is moved when we cry out to him during our trials and ask him for wisdom and comfort. Let us set aside time each day to worship him. Let us sing to him and recall all he has done for us in Christ. Let us ponder his word. Let us ask Jesus to deliver us from our sins and free us to serve him. Whenever we spend time with Jesus, we have his full attention. He is never distracted or in a hurry. He waits for us to come and talk with him. He longs to tell us his thoughts and give us his love.

"Jesus, you have set me free by your death and resurrection. I praise you! I give my life to you. Thank you for your immense love for me."

Healing, Persecution, and Progress

ACTS
3–5

Acts 3:1-10

[1] Now Peter and John were going up to the temple at the hour of prayer, the ninth hour. [2] And a man lame from birth was being carried, whom they laid daily at that gate of the temple which is called Beautiful to ask alms of those who entered the temple. [3] Seeing Peter and John about to go into the temple, he asked for alms. [4] And Peter directed his gaze at him, with John, and said, "Look at us." [5] And he fixed his attention upon them, expecting to receive something from them. [6] But Peter said, "I have no silver and gold, but I give you what I have; in the name of Jesus Christ of Nazareth, walk." [7] And he took him by the right hand and raised him up; and immediately his feet and ankles were made strong. [8] And leaping up he stood and walked and entered the temple with them, walking and leaping and praising God. [9] And all the people saw him walking and praising God, [10] and recognized him as the one who sat for alms at the Beautiful Gate of the temple; and they were filled with wonder and amazement at what had happened to him. ✍

Whenever sick people came to Jesus in faith, they were healed. He healed those who were spiritually sick (needing deliverance or forgiveness of sin) and those who were physically ill (the lame, the blind, the lepers). Sickness was a manifestation of the kingdom of Satan that Jesus had come to destroy.

The early church continued to act as Christ had. The apostles proclaimed the gospel and many healings took place. The man who had been crippled from birth (Acts 3:2) probably had long since given up any hope of being healed. But Peter, confident of the power of the name of Jesus, said to him: "I have no silver and gold, but I give you what I have; in the name of Jesus Christ of Nazareth, walk" (3:6). The crippled man not only walked, he went with Peter and John to the temple, leaping about and praising God.

It was always God's intention to have all people share his life. We are often like the crippled man begging at the temple gate; we too need an inner assurance of God's love and a deeper awareness of his power to change our lives. But the good news of Jesus has transformed the world, bringing healing and life to all who will receive.

Peter had preached on Pentecost at the temple in Jerusalem of "signs on the earth" (a reference to the prophecy of Joel 2:28-32) made possible by God who poured out his Spirit upon all flesh (Acts 2:17,19). The death and resurrection of Jesus and the sending of the Holy Spirit have unleashed a great spiritual power on the earth. This miracle of the healing of the man lame from birth was a sign of that power and testimony to the fulfillment of the prophecy of Joel.

Jesus' own ministry reflected signs of God's power: "The blind receive their sight, the lame walk, lepers are cleansed, the deaf hear, the dead are raised, and the poor have the good news brought to them" (Matthew 11:5). This speaks of power, deliverance, and healing—and these things happen through the power of the Holy Spirit.

What should the healing of the lame man mean for us? Should we too expect healing through the power of God? The truth is that God does heal to reveal his love, presence, and power. Many shrines throughout the world give testimony to this power through crutches left behind as evidence of God's gracious love: Lourdes in France, Einsiedeln in Switzerland, Mission Hill in the United States, St. Joseph's Oratory in Canada, to name a few.

But more importantly, this account should fix in our minds the truth that great spiritual power is released through the death and resurrection of Jesus and the sending of the Spirit of God. This story should help to increase our expectation that God can and *does* act in human lives for our own sake and for the sake of the whole church.

"Lord Jesus, send forth your Spirit and renew the face of the earth."

Acts 3:11-26

[11] While he clung to Peter and John, all the people ran together to them in the portico called Solomon's, astounded. [12] And when Peter saw it he addressed the people, "Men of Israel, why do you wonder at this, or why do you stare at us, as though by our own power or piety we had made him walk? [13] The God of Abraham and of Isaac and of Jacob, the God of our fathers, glorified his servant Jesus, whom you delivered up and denied in the presence of Pilate, when he had decided to release him. [14] But you denied the Holy and Righteous One, and asked for a murderer to be granted to you, [15] and killed the Author of life, whom God raised from the dead. To this we are witnesses. [16] And his name, by faith in his name, has made this man strong whom you see and know; and the faith which is through Jesus has given the man this perfect health in the presence of you all.

[17] "And now, brethren, I know that you acted in ignorance, as did also your rulers. [18] But what God foretold by the mouth of all the prophets, that his Christ should suffer, he thus fulfilled. [19] Repent therefore, and turn again, that your sins may be blotted out, that times of refreshing may come from the presence of the Lord, [20] and that he may send the Christ appointed for you, Jesus, [21] whom heaven must receive until the time for establishing all that God spoke by the mouth of his holy prophets from of old. [22] Moses said, 'The Lord God will raise up for you a prophet from your brethren as he raised me up. You shall listen to him in whatever he tells you. [23] And it shall be that every soul that does not listen to that prophet shall be destroyed from the people.' [24] And all the prophets who have spoken, from Samuel and those who came afterwards, also proclaimed these days. [25] You are the sons of the prophets and of the covenant which God gave to your fathers, saying to Abraham, 'And in your posterity shall all the families of the earth be blessed.' [26] God, having raised up his servant, sent him to you first, to bless you in turning every one of you from your wickedness."

I magine what it would be like to see someone miraculously healed! We might be struck by God's sovereign power and mercy or we might just stand in amazement. We might be curious, wanting to know more, or we might experience total disbelief. This was what happened when the Lord healed the lame man at the temple through Peter and John. Miracles, signs, and wonders always cause people to ask questions. They did in Peter and John's lifetime; they do today. God uses our questions to draw us closer to him so that we can experience the "times of refreshing" spoken of by Peter (Acts 3:19).

God longs for us to know the refreshment of his presence. When we turn our lives over to Jesus, the Holy Spirit inaugurates an entirely new life in us. Through Jesus, we can experience relief from the burdens that have weighed us down. Guilt and depression, sadness and sorrow, anger and hurt can melt away as we come to know God's merciful love and forgiveness. No sin, no matter how great, is unforgivable if we will turn to Jesus and ask him into our lives to save and forgive us. This forgiveness is ours for the asking.

Once we have experienced such life-changing mercy, God continues to offer us his refreshment. Even in the space of one day, we can become terribly burdened by sin and the trials of everyday life. But our loving Father longs to lift our burdens and reconcile us to himself. As we turn to the indwelling Holy Spirit each day, he will give us light to see our sins and grace to turn from them.

Let us ask God to open our hearts and draw us close. He wants us to know the refreshment of his presence. Let us commit our lives to Jesus and allow the Holy Spirit to begin a new life in us. We can turn to Jesus each day, asking him into our lives, bringing his love and mercy. God wants us, his precious children, to come to him each day, repentant and open to his grace.

"Holy Spirit, apart from your light, we cannot see our failings. Give us the grace to turn from sin so that we might come into the presence of God and be refreshed every day."

Acts 4:1-12

[1] And as they were speaking to the people, the priests and the captain of the temple and the Sadducees came upon them, [2] annoyed because they were teaching the people and proclaiming in Jesus the resurrection from the dead. [3] And they arrested them and put them in custody until the morrow, for it was already evening. [4] But many of those who heard the word believed; and the number of the men came to about five thousand. [5] On the morrow their rulers and elders and scribes were gathered together in Jerusalem, [6] with Annas the high priest and Caiaphas and John and Alexander, and all who were of the high-priestly family. [7] And when they had set them in the midst, they inquired, "By what power or by what name did you do this?" [8] Then Peter, filled with the Holy Spirit, said to them, "Rulers of the people and elders, [9] if we are being examined today concerning a good deed done to a cripple, by what means this man has been healed, [10] be it known to you all, and to all the people of Israel, that by the name of Jesus Christ of Nazareth, whom you crucified, whom God raised from the dead, by him this man is standing before you well. [11] This is the stone which was rejected by you builders, but which has become the head of the corner. [12] And there is salvation in no one else, for there is no other name under heaven given among men by which we must be saved."

The two apostles caused quite a commotion when—in the name of Jesus—they healed the crippled man in the temple (Acts 3:1-10). They caught the attention of the people as well as the authorities. In short order, they were thrown in jail, then taken before the religious leaders to make an explanation. The members of the Sanhedrin—and especially the Sadducees (whose denial that there was a life after death was directly challenged by the rising of Jesus)—were determined to curb this development before it got out of hand.

Many people and societies have held strong beliefs about the importance of a name. "In whose name?" translates to mean, "By whose power?" It is not surprising, therefore, that the Sanhedrin demanded to know in whose name or by what power Peter and John had performed this act. The two disciples were as candid with the Sanhedrin as they had been with the crowd at the temple: "By the name of Jesus Christ of Nazareth, whom you crucified, whom God raised from the dead, by him this man is standing before you well" (Acts 4:10).

When they told the lame man, "In the name of Jesus Christ of Nazareth, walk" (Acts 3:6), they invoked the power of Jesus himself. The Sanhedrin would have known this as well; they realized that if this sort of thing were allowed to continue, there would be no stopping it. The potential repercussions were all too obvious. Peter finished his speech with one final truth, "There is salvation in no one else, for there is no other name under heaven given among men by which we must be saved" (Acts 4:12).

We cannot fail to note Peter's absolute faith in the name of Jesus. He knew the power in this name and he called upon it. We can learn from this example and do likewise. Whether we are held back by fear, timidity, resentments, jealousy, anger, or by any spirit that is not of the Lord, we have the capacity through the Holy Spirit to conquer it and to cast it out in Jesus' name. Let us stand in faith upon the power and authority of the name of Jesus to heal the infirmities that cripple the world.

"Lord Jesus, I trust absolutely in the power and authority of your name. I will call upon your name for my every need, and for the needs of all your children. Lord, I praise your holy name!"

Acts 4:13-22

[13] Now when they saw the boldness of Peter and John, and perceived that they were uneducated, common men, they wondered; and they recognized that they had been with Jesus. [14] But seeing the man that had been healed standing beside them, they had nothing to say in opposition. [15] But when they had commanded them to go aside out of the council, they conferred with one another, [16] saying, "What shall we do with these men? For that a notable sign has been performed through them is manifest to all the inhabitants of Jerusalem, and we cannot deny it. [17] But in order that it may spread no further among the people, let us warn them to speak no more to any one in this name." [18] So they called them and charged them not to speak or teach at all in the name of Jesus. [19] But Peter and John answered them, "Whether it is right in the sight of God to listen to you rather than to God, you must judge; [20] for we cannot but speak of what we have seen and heard." [21] And when they had further threatened them, they let them go, finding no way to punish them, because of the people; for all men praised God for what had happened. [22] For the man on whom this sign of healing was performed was more than forty years old.

Dramatic changes took place in the apostles, especially Peter, as reported in the early chapters of Acts. As we read about them, we may marvel at the boldness, courage, and power that is reflected in Peter, and still wonder if this change could happen in our lives. "After all," we might reason, "Peter was an apostle but I am just an ordinary person. What do I know about religious things?"

We tend to forget that this is what Peter and John were—"uneducated, common men" (Acts 4:13). God does not demand that we be spiritual experts with special gifts in order for the Spirit to work in our lives. The only requirements are that we believe in Jesus and want to be obedient to his commandments. If this is our desire, we will see the power of God work in our lives just as it did in Peter's life. We just need to ask the Holy Spirit to use us as witnesses to Jesus during each day.

The ability to speak about the work of God did not come to Peter and John through some sort of magical force. Instead, it grew and developed in them as they were faithful to God. They—like the early converts to Christ—devoted themselves to "teaching and fellowship, to the breaking of bread and the prayers" (Acts 2:42). They pondered all they had "seen and heard" (4:20) regarding the life, death, and res-urrection of Jesus and spoke about it as it burned in their hearts. In a similar way, we will grow in the ability to speak about the work of God through Christ Jesus.

The scribes and the Pharisees were staunch opponents of Jesus and his followers. Even so, they had to acknowledge the mirac-ulous work of God in healing the crippled beggar (Acts 4:16). Both within the church and without, what is most needed today is an authentic and powerful witness by God's people to the changing and healing power of the gospel. In our homes and neighborhoods, in our schools, in our jobs, and in our churches, God is calling his people— even the ordinary and uneducated—to let the Holy Spirit make us pow-erful witnesses to Christ.

Today, let us decide to accept his call to be witnesses to Christ by responding to the opportunities that we encounter to share our faith with those we meet.

Acts 4:23-31

23 When they were released they went to their friends and reported what the chief priests and the elders had said to them. 24 And when they heard it, they lifted their voices together to God and said, "Sovereign Lord, who didst make the heaven and the earth and the sea and everything in them, 25 who by the mouth of our father David, thy servant, didst say by the Holy Spirit, 'Why did the Gentiles rage, and the peoples imagine vain things? 26 The kings of the earth set themselves in array, and the rulers were gathered together, against the Lord and against his Anointed'— 27 for truly in this city there were gathered together against thy holy servant Jesus, whom thou didst anoint, both Herod and Pontius Pilate, with the Gentiles and the peoples of Israel, 28 to do whatever thy hand and thy plan had predestined to take place. 29 And now, Lord, look upon their threats, and grant to thy servants to speak thy word with all boldness, 30 while thou stretchest out thy hand to heal, and signs and wonders are performed through the name of thy holy servant Jesus." 31 And when they had prayed, the place in which they were gathered together was shaken; and they were all filled with the Holy Spirit and spoke the word of God with boldness.

How would you react after being hauled before the authorities and threatened because of your faith in Christ? Would you speak out loudly against their hardness of heart? Would you complain about the injustice done to you? Would you seek revenge? Or, would you seek out your brothers and sisters and pray with them? This is what Peter and John did, and their prayer was one of expectation, trust, and power.

In this prayer, we get a glimpse into the disciples' hearts as they faced hardship for the sake of the gospel. Despite the persecution and the threat of more severe reprisals, they were determined to obey the Lord and proclaim the good news. Rather than taking their difficulties as a sign that they should stop, they came to a prophetic understanding of their situation through Scripture, and they drew confidence that God was indeed with them.

Because of their humble trust and confidence in the Lord, the disciples had the courage to ask God to continue pouring out signs and wonders that would only get them into deeper trouble! But they knew that God wanted to reveal himself through them, and so they trusted in him and asked for an increase in power.

Dietrich Bonhoeffer, a Lutheran pastor in Germany who was arrested—and ultimately executed—for taking a stand against Hitler's regime, is a modern example of one whose trust in the Lord enabled him to face persecution with patience and faith. Not long before his execution, he described his disposition in a letter to a close friend:

> Please don't ever get anxious or worried about me, but don't forget to pray for me—I'm sure you don't! I am so sure of God's guiding hand that I hope I shall always be kept in that certainty. You must never doubt that I'm traveling with gratitude and cheerfulness along the road where I'm being led. My past life is brim-full of God's goodness, and my sins are covered by the forgiving love of Christ crucified. I'm most thankful for the people I have met, and I only hope that they never have to grieve about me, but that they, too, will always be certain of, and thankful for, God's mercy and forgiveness. (Letter to Eberhard Bethge, August 23, 1944)

"Lord Jesus, help us to place our lives completely in your hands. Teach us that with you we can face every situation with courage and hope."

Acts 4:32-37

32 Now the company of those who believed were of one heart and soul, and no one said that any of the things which he possessed was his own, but they had everything in common. 33 And with great power the apostles gave their testimony to the resurrection of the Lord Jesus, and great grace was upon them all. 34 There was not a needy person among them, for as many as were possessors of lands or houses sold them, and brought the proceeds of what was sold 35 and laid it at the apostles' feet; and distribution was made to each as any had need. 36 Thus Joseph who was surnamed by the apostles Barnabas (which means, Son of encouragement), a Levite, a native of Cyprus, 37 sold a field which belonged to him, and brought the money and laid it at the apostles' feet. ✺

From the moment the Father created humanity, he intended that we be united to himself and to each other. When we fell into sin, he sent his Son Jesus, not only to save us, but also to restore the intrinsic unity the Father had planned for us.

The world witnessed the fulfillment of God's plan in the lives of the first Christians. "Now the whole group of those who believed were of one heart and soul, and no one claimed private ownership of any possessions, but everything they owned was held in common.... There was not a needy person among them" (Acts 4:32,34).

Love and fellowship characterized the early church and marked it as the fruit of God's work. The church is called to display the same unity in every generation. In our own day, the Second Vatican Council proclaimed:

God has willed to make men holy and save them, not as individuals without any bond or link between them, but rather to make them into a people who might acknowledge him and serve him in holiness. . . . All men are called to belong to the new People of God. This People, therefore, whilst remaining one and only one, is to be spread throughout the whole world and to all ages in order that the design of God's will may be fulfilled. (*Lumen Gentium*, 9,13)

Is the unity to which we are called by the Scriptures and the Second Vatican Council realistic? Is it possible? No. . . . That is, *until* and *unless* we yield to God's resurrection life. The disciples quarreled and bickered even when Jesus was with them. Only after he died and rose again were they able to yield to the Holy Spirit's transforming power.

We all know the bitter reality of being hurt or betrayed by others, even by those in our own families and churches. But God's love and healing are just as real. We can approach God and submit our failings to his divine power through personal prayer and the sacraments. In faith we wait for the ultimate reality when the new Jerusalem will be established in complete and eternal union.

"Father, you earnestly desire that your people become one in your Son. Teach us to seek after this unity that is so dear to your heart. Through your Spirit of love, give us this same yearning in our hearts."

Acts 5:1-11

[1] But a man named Ananias with his wife Sapphira sold a piece of property, [2] and with his wife's knowledge he kept back some of the proceeds, and brought only a part and laid it at the apostles' feet. [3] But Peter said, "Ananias, why has Satan filled your heart to lie to the Holy Spirit and to keep back part of the proceeds of the land? [4] While it remained unsold, did it not remain your own? And after it was sold, was it not at your disposal? How is it that you have contrived this deed in your heart? You have not lied to men but to God." [5] When Ananias heard these words, he fell down and died. And great fear came upon all who heard of it. [6] The young men rose and wrapped him up and carried him out and buried him. [7] After an interval of about three hours his wife came in, not knowing what had happened. [8] And Peter said to her, "Tell me whether you sold the land for so much." And she said, "Yes, for so much." [9] But Peter said to her, "How is it that you have agreed together to tempt the Spirit of the Lord? Hark, the feet of those that have buried your husband are at the door, and they will carry you out." [10] Immediately she fell down at his feet and died. When the young men came in they found her dead, and they carried her out and buried her beside her husband. [11] And great fear came upon the whole church, and upon all who heard of these things. ᴈ

In telling the story of Ananias and Sapphira, Luke wisely placed it immediately after his story about the generosity of Barnabas. The contrast couldn't be greater. Barnabas, whom Luke described later as a man "full of the Holy Spirit" (Acts 11:24), was exceedingly generous. Ananias, on the other hand, let his heart be filled with Satan and put on only a show of generosity.

St. Luke told these stories to demonstrate the difference between how listening to Satan or to the Holy Spirit changes the way we act. Having sold a field and donated the money to help the poor, Barnabas demon-strated how the Spirit enabled him to be generous, united with his broth-ers and sisters, and honest with the apostles. Ananias, on the other hand, acted hypocritically, lied to Peter and to God, and broke the unity of the community. As Peter pointed out, Ananias didn't have to give any money to the apostles. Perhaps only because he wanted to look good in the eyes of his brothers and sisters, Ananias hatched a deceptive plot that would boost his reputation but keep him wealthy.

Luke's point in contrasting these two men is clear. We too can choose whether we want to open our hearts to the Holy Spirit or listen to the lies of the devil. We don't have to worry about being controlled by the devil if we are honestly seeking God. As Luke wrote in his gospel, our Father in heaven gives the Holy Spirit generously to anyone who asks him (Luke 11:13). The story of Ananias is not meant to make us more afraid of the devil. It's meant to make us more eager for the Holy Spirit. It's not meant to fill us with dread, but give us hope that through the Spirit we can be delivered of every sin—even sins big enough to cause a condemnation like Ananias'.

Let us ask for more of the Spirit in our lives. Let us listen for his promptings. He lives within us and wants to lead, teach, and strengthen us. With practice we can learn to distinguish his voice from the philoso-phies of the world and the lies of the devil. The Spirit loves us and wants to relate to us in a free and easy way. We can experiment by asking the Spirit for guidance and expecting an answer. Maybe we will want to start on small things and gradually move on to bolder things—always being careful to discern these leadings with wise and mature Christians like our parish priest or a trusted spiritual director. The more we learn to listen to the Spirit, the more we will resemble Barnabas, Peter, John, and all the first Christians who dedicated their hearts to loving and serving Jesus.

"Thank you, Holy Spirit. You never tire of speaking to my heart. Keep coming, Holy Spirit."

Acts 5:12-16

[12] Now many signs and wonders were done among the people by the hands of the apostles. And they were all together in Solomon's Portico. [13] None of the rest dared join them, but the people held them in high honor. [14] And more than ever believers were added to the Lord, multitudes both of men and women, [15] so that they even carried out the sick into the streets, and laid them on beds and pallets, that as Peter came by at least his shadow might fall on some of them. [16] The people also gathered from the towns around Jerusalem, bringing the sick and those afflicted with unclean spirits, and they were all healed.

The power that Peter and the apostles and all the other Christians experienced in the early church is still with us! It is the power of the Holy Spirit, whom Jesus promised to everyone who believes in him. Are you experiencing this power actively in your life? What about in your home, school, or parish? Is your experience of the power of the Spirit something that is constantly growing and changing? It's good to ask these questions every now and then. Jesus always wants to take us deeper into his life, but he won't do it without our cooperation.

How easy it can be to accept a reduced experience of Christianity. How easy to think that we're not supposed to expect the kind of miracles that the first Christians witnessed. How tempting it can be to resign ourselves to a life that is only partially touched by the love of God. Yet, the same Holy Spirit is in us as he was in Peter, Mary, and John. He never changes. The power of God available to us is just as great today as it was in the Book of Acts.

In the end, it all boils down to a question of faith. Do you believe that God actually does want to heal, deliver, and pour out his power in you and through you? Remember, Jesus had to encourage his own disciples over and over again to have more faith. He wants all of us to have the kind of faith that can move mountains. He wants all of us to walk in the dynamic expectancy that we can experience the power of the Holy Spirit in our lives.

How do we increase our faith? First, we should simply pray for it. Jesus told us to ask, seek, and knock. He delights in giving us more faith. Second, it often helps to establish trusted relationships with other people with the same goals, especially those who may even be a little farther along than we are. Often, faith "jumps" from one believer to another, and those who are walking in greater faith can help to increase our faith. Third, read, study, and ponder the Scriptures, especially this Book of Acts. The word of God has the power to transform our lives and increase our faith, too!

"Lord, I praise you for your all-encompassing power. Increase my faith, and help me to experience more of the Holy Spirit in my life."

Acts 5:17-26

[17] But the high priest rose up and all who were with him, that is, the party of the Sadducees, and filled with jealousy [18] they arrested the apostles and put them in the common prison. [19] But at night an angel of the Lord opened the prison doors and brought them out and said, [20] "Go and stand in the temple and speak to the people all the words of this Life." [21] And when they heard this, they entered the temple at daybreak and taught.

Now the high priest came and those who were with him and called together the council and all the senate of Israel, and sent to the prison to have them brought. [22] But when the officers came, they did not find them in the prison, and they returned and reported, [23] "We found the prison securely locked and the sentries standing at the doors, but when we opened it we found no one inside." [24] Now when the captain of the temple and the chief priests heard these words, they were much perplexed about them, wondering what this would come to. [25] And some one came and told them, "The men whom you put in prison are standing in the temple and teaching the people." [26] Then the captain with the officers went and brought them, but without violence, for they were afraid of being stoned by the people.

I t was in obedience to the Lord's instructions (Matthew 28:19; Acts 1:8) that the disciples preached the good news in Jerusalem. Even when the chief priests and elders ordered them to stop (Acts 4:17), the disciples chose to obey God rather than human authorities. Because of that decision, they were thrown into prison.

The word "obedience" in our English versions of Scripture is usually a translation of the Greek work *hypakoe'*, itself a compound of *akoe'*, "to hear, to listen," and *hypo*, "to put oneself under [what is heard]." Sometimes "obedience" is a translation of *peithomai*, "to let oneself be persuaded, to trust." In both cases, obedience is not a passive giving up of one's own ideas, but an active response to cooperate with something heard. This is what the disciples were doing. They were cooperating with Jesus' words and the promptings of the Holy Spirit.

In the same way, we are called to be obedient to God, not just by giving up our own ideas—though this may often be the result—but by responding to what we hear from God and trusting him. Such obedience involves our stepping out in faith and seeking to help others rather than ourselves.

It may not be easy to help the homeless or the hungry in our communities, particularly if it is at the expense of something we would dearly like to have for ourselves. It may not be easy to respond to the call for more prayer or Scripture reading when so many projects are crying to be done. It may not be easy to spend time relating to someone in need rather than watching our favorite television program. Nor was it easy for the disciples to go back to preaching (Acts 5:20-21), the very act for which they had been jailed. Yet we know God blessed their obedience and used it to build his church.

Christ's resurrection must have an impact on our lives. If we truly believe that he is risen and glorified, we must be obedient to his call; we need to seek and respond to the Holy Spirit's promptings. Let us ask for the grace to understand what it means to be obedient to Christ.

Acts 5:27-33

²⁷ And when they had brought them, they set them before the council. And the high priest questioned them, ²⁸ saying, "We strictly charged you not to teach in this name, yet here you have filled Jerusalem with your teaching and you intend to bring this man's blood upon us." ²⁹ But Peter and the apostles answered, "We must obey God rather than men. ³⁰ The God of our fathers raised Jesus whom you killed by hanging him on a tree. ³¹ God exalted him at his right hand as Leader and Savior, to give repentance to Israel and forgiveness of sins. ³² And we are witnesses to these things, and so is the Holy Spirit whom God has given to those who obey him."
³³ When they heard this they were enraged and wanted to kill them.

The God of our fathers raised Jesus whom you killed. (Acts 5:30)

Not long before this encounter with the Sanhedrin, Peter had come face-to-face with his own role in the event leading up to Jesus' death. He had told Jesus that he would rather die than deny him, yet hours later he did in fact deny Jesus, three times (Luke 22:31-34,54-61). Realizing what he had done, Peter broke down and wept (22:62). At that point, he could have run away or drowned in his own guilt. Instead, Peter chose to repent. He acknowledged his sin, took responsibility for it, and humbly allowed God to cleanse him. He didn't defend himself or try to avoid Jesus' searching gaze. And, as a result, Peter knew true freedom and consolation from heaven.

With this background, we can understand why Peter was so eager to speak to the people in the temple about Jesus (Acts 5:17-21). Knowing the joy of God's forgiveness, Peter wanted others to experience it too— even the members of the religious council in charge of the temple. But he knew that, if they were going to experience the freedom he knew, they too had to acknowledge their sin and come to repentance. They had to admit that, just like Peter, they too were responsible for Jesus' death. And so, Peter pleaded with them as fellow sinners to embrace the repentance that leads to life.

In a sense, each of us shares responsibility for the death of Jesus, since it was to atone for our sins that he died. Yet like the Sanhedrin (Acts 5:28), we can find it hard to own up to our sins. We tend to blame others. We want to run away. We minimize our responsibility. But none of these strategies brings us real freedom. The only way out is to follow Peter's example, acknowledge our guilt, and turn to Jesus for mercy.

God very much wants to forgive us. That was the whole point of Peter's words to the Sanhedrin. He hoped that everyone—even his enemies—would become like him, sinners set free by the mercy of a crucified and risen Savior.

"Lord Jesus, thank you for dying on the cross to redeem me from sin, guilt, and shame. I acknowledge that it was my sin that killed you, and I humbly accept the forgiveness that you won for me."

Acts 5:34-42

34 But a Pharisee in the council named Gamali-el, a teacher of the law, held in honor by all the people, stood up and ordered the men to be put outside for a while. 35 And he said to them, "Men of Israel, take care what you do with these men. 36 For before these days Theudas arose, giving himself out to be somebody, and a number of men, about four hundred, joined him; but he was slain and all who followed him were dispersed and came to nothing. 37 After him Judas the Galilean arose in the days of the census and drew away some of the people after him; he also perished, and all who followed him were scattered. 38 So in the present case I tell you, keep away from these men and let them alone; for if this plan or this undertaking is of men, it will fail; 39 but if it is of God, you will not be able to overthrow them. You might even be found opposing God!"

40 So they took his advice, and when they had called in the apostles, they beat them and charged them not to speak in the name of Jesus, and let them go. 41 Then they left the presence of the council, rejoicing that they were counted worthy to suffer dishonor for the name. 42 And every day in the temple and at home they did not cease teaching and preaching Jesus as the Christ.

How could the apostles rejoice just after having been beaten by Jewish soldiers? Scripture tells us that it was because they were deemed worthy to suffer dishonor for Jesus (Acts 5:41). They were grateful to experience the Holy Spirit's power enabling them to teach and preach about Jesus, despite opposition and persecution. Would you rejoice in these circumstances? Maybe you would if you knew for certain that God had called you to do the thing that had landed you in so much trouble. This certainly was the apostles' conviction. They knew that the Lord had a calling for their lives.

Jesus promised the apostles that when the Holy Spirit came upon them, they would be his witnesses (Acts 1:8). They rejoiced because the Holy Spirit had filled them—and continued to fill them—with the strength and courage to do what they were called to do. Their dedication to preaching the gospel was not of human origin alone—it was also from a spiritual source.

Every one of us is invited to receive the same power of the Spirit that the disciples manifested. Every one of us can become Jesus' witnesses in the roles that we have been given and in the tasks that we must fulfill. As we turn to the Spirit and ask him how he wants us to use our gifts, and as we seek the Lord's plan for our lives, we will begin to know the Spirit's power and strength. We will no longer be relying only upon our own natural talents. We can draw from the limitless resources of the One who dwells within us.

Some of us are called to preach the gospel, others to care for the poor. Perhaps we are called simply to be a good parent, a peaceful coworker, or a neighbor who brings the light of Christ to those around us. Yet, in each of these callings, we can be like the early apostles who constantly witnessed and taught about Jesus. Today, let us ask Jesus for the grace to obey the Holy Spirit and share the love of God with everyone we encounter.

"Father, we praise you for your divine wisdom and for your loving plan of life and salvation for each and every person. Let your love and grace shine through us for all the world to see."

The First Martyr

ACTS
6:1–8:1

Acts 6:1-7

[1] Now in these days when the disciples were increasing in number, the Hellenists murmured against the Hebrews because their widows were neglected in the daily distribution. [2] And the twelve summoned the body of the disciples and said, "It is not right that we should give up preaching the word of God to serve tables. [3] Therefore, brethren, pick out from among you seven men of good repute, full of the Spirit and of wisdom, whom we may appoint to this duty. [4] But we will devote ourselves to prayer and to the ministry of the word." [5] And what they said pleased the whole multitude, and they chose Stephen, a man full of faith and of the Holy Spirit, and Philip, and Prochorus, and Nicanor, and Timon, and Parmenas, and Nicolaus, a proselyte of Antioch.
[6] These they set before the apostles, and they prayed and laid their hands upon them.
[7] And the word of God increased; and the number of the disciples multiplied greatly in Jerusalem, and a great many of the priests were obedient to the faith.

The apostles wanted to devote themselves exclusively "to prayer and to the ministry of the word" (Acts 6:4). But what was this "word" to which they wanted to devote all their time? For the apostles—who lived with Jesus, saw him die, and then marveled at his resurrection—the "ministry of the word" meant telling people about Jesus.

We need to be careful not to read this passage only with our twenty-first-century eyes. The apostles were not simply committed to studying the Scriptures and talking about them with people. Of course, they knew and shared Scripture with others, but the primary "word" they proclaimed was their personal knowledge of Jesus Christ. The apostles had been friends of Jesus. They had traveled throughout Palestine with him.

They had seen and touched his risen body. They saw him ascend into heaven. For them, "ministry of the word" was a commitment to tell others about their relationship with Jesus and about the new life that everyone can experience through a similar relationship with the Lord.

The connection to our lives is clear: We can know Jesus in the same way that the apostles did. They did not just know *about* Jesus; they *knew* him. And, just as the apostles heralded their message to the world, so can we. After Jesus ascended into heaven, the Holy Spirit continued to make Jesus known to the apostles in ever more intimate ways by sending his love to fill their hearts and his wisdom to illuminate their minds. As a result, wherever they went, Jesus became the "word" that they ministered.

Do you know Jesus personally? Do you read Scripture with an expectation that you can develop a close and loving relationship with him? Scripture can bring us in touch not only with the teachings and philosophies of Jesus, but with Jesus himself. Let us take up the ministry of the word of God as we read Scripture prayerfully, with open hearts, asking the Holy Spirit to bring Jesus ever closer to us. As we do, Jesus will become our intimate friend.

"Holy Spirit, help me come closer to Jesus. Speak, Lord, for your servant is listening. Help me to listen carefully for the voice of God. Give me the grace to share this 'word' with everyone I know."

Acts 6:8-15

[8] And Stephen, full of grace and power, did great wonders and signs among the people. [9] Then some of those who belonged to the synagogue of the Freedmen (as it was called), and of the Cyrenians, and of the Alexandrians, and of those from Cilicia and Asia, arose and disputed with Stephen. [10] But they could not withstand the wisdom and the Spirit with which he spoke. [11] Then they secretly instigated men, who said, "We have heard him speak blasphemous words against Moses and God." [12] And they stirred up the people and the elders and the scribes, and they came upon him and seized him and brought him before the council, [13] and set up false witnesses who said, "This man never ceases to speak words against this holy place and the law; [14] for we have heard him say that this Jesus of Nazareth will destroy this place, and will change the customs which Moses delivered to us." [15] And gazing at him, all who sat in the council saw that his face was like the face of an angel. ✍

Stephen was one of seven good men chosen to see to the needs of the Greek-speaking community at Jerusalem, helping with food distribution and waiting on tables. The apostles recognized the importance of this task and felt that it required men "full of the Spirit and of wisdom" (Acts 6:3). This position of service apparently constituted no obstacle for Stephen—and may even have afforded him a vehicle—in his zeal to proclaim the good news. He quickly became a recognized figure in the holy city, admired and respected by those who found life in his words, hated and feared by those who were blind to the truth.

Luke described Stephen as a man "full of grace and power, [who] did great wonders and signs among the people" (Acts 6:8). When the doubters and detractors engaged him in debate, "they could not withstand the wisdom and the Spirit with which he spoke" (6:10). Clearly, Stephen was a man in whom the Spirit worked in power, a man who had given himself over totally to the task of spreading the word of God.

Where did Stephen find his driving power of evangelism? How did he become so committed to caring for the needs of the disadvantaged church? Stephen had been selected by members of the community because of his apparent virtues and, along with six others, was presented to the apostles for their blessing and approval. The apostles "prayed and laid their hands upon them" (Acts 6:6). This was the customary manner in the early church by which people were invested with the power of the Holy Spirit to carry out special assignments. From this prayer of petition to the Lord and the laying on of hands came the infilling of the Spirit and the empowerment to serve the Lord (see also Acts 13:1-3).

Without the enabling of the Holy Spirit, our services to the Lord are always limited by our own human potential. Good works performed out of human capabilities and human leadings will always achieve only human goals. Ask your Christian brothers and sisters to pray *with* you and *for* you that the Holy Spirit will become a limitless source of zeal and energy to enable you to do the work of God—in your family, your church, and your workplace.

Acts 7:1-16

[1] And the high priest said, "Is this so?" [2] And Stephen said: "Brethren and fathers, hear me. The God of glory appeared to our father Abraham, when he was in Mesopotamia, before he lived in Haran, [3] and said to him, 'Depart from your land and from your kindred and go into the land which I will show you.' [4] Then he departed from the land of the Chaldeans, and lived in Haran. And after his father died, God removed him from there into this land in which you are now living; [5] yet he gave him no inheritance in it, not even a foot's length, but promised to give it to him in possession and to his posterity after him, though he had no child. [6] And God spoke to this effect, that his posterity would be aliens in a land belonging to others, who would enslave them and ill-treat them four hundred years. [7] 'But I will judge the nation which they serve,' said God, 'and after that they shall come out and worship me in this place.' [8] And he gave him the covenant of circumcision. And so Abraham became the father of Isaac, and circumcised him on the eighth day; and Isaac became the father of Jacob, and Jacob of the twelve patriarchs.
[9] "And the patriarchs, jealous of Joseph, sold him into Egypt; but God was with him, [10] and rescued him out of all his afflictions, and gave him favor and wisdom before Pharaoh, king of Egypt, who made him governor over Egypt and over all his household. [11] Now there came a famine throughout all Egypt and Canaan, and great affliction, and our fathers could find no food. [12] But when Jacob heard that there was grain in Egypt, he sent forth our fathers the first time. [13] And at the second visit Joseph made himself known to his brothers, and Joseph's family became known to Pharaoh. [14] And Joseph sent and called to him Jacob his father and all his kindred, seventy-five souls; [15] and Jacob went down into Egypt. And he died, himself and our fathers, [16] and they were carried back to Shechem and laid in the tomb that Abraham had bought for a sum of silver from the sons of Hamor in Shechem."

S tephen was accused of speaking blasphemies against Moses and God (Acts 6:11). Angry, jealous men had incited the people, the elders, and the scribes against him. They dragged Stephen before the Sanhedrin and brought in false witnesses, who claimed that he had denounced the temple and the law (6:14). Then, just as they had done to Jesus, they rejected and killed him (7:58-60).

Stephen wanted the Sanhedrin to know that Jesus truly was the long-awaited Messiah, but he was aware that even the name of Jesus would fill them with rage. So he began instead by speaking about things he knew they wouldn't reject outright: their ancestors and their history. By recounting their history, Stephen sought to show them that from the very beginning, God was working with a purpose in mind—and that this purpose was fulfilled in Christ.

Like Abraham and the early Hebrews about whom Stephen spoke, we too are on a pilgrimage. God is continually leading us out of bondage into a place where we can worship freely. Sometimes, we may be called to radical obedience, as was Abraham, who had to leave home and family to go to a place he knew nothing about (Genesis 12:1). We may experience trials or sufferings like the patriarch Joseph. Or we may simply experience a call to take the next step of obedience that will lead us to a deeper level of knowing God.

Regardless of the circumstances, when we are called, our answer must be that of Abraham, whose faith was counted as righteousness (Genesis 15:6). The key to obeying God is faith—trusting God's promises, even when it looks as though they could not possibly come true. The key is believing, even when nothing makes sense, and putting our faith in God absolutely. It means not having a safety net or a "Plan B" in case he fails. After all, our faith tells us he won't!

Our God is a generous God. We can increase our faith by testing the little bit of faith we know we do have. We can exercise it and watch it strengthen and grow—all the time asking for more faith. That's one prayer God never tires of answering!

"Father, I believe you will give good things to me, just as you promised. Give me faith as strong as Abraham's and Stephen's, and strengthen the faith I already have, so that I may walk with you today and every day."

Acts 7:17-43

[17] "But as the time of the promise drew near, which God had granted to Abraham, the people grew and multiplied in Egypt [18] till there arose over Egypt another king who had not known Joseph. [19] He dealt craftily with our race and forced our fathers to expose their infants, that they might not be kept alive. [20] At this time Moses was born, and was beautiful before God. And he was brought up for three months in his father's house; [21] and when he was exposed, Pharaoh's daughter adopted him and brought him up as her own son. [22] And Moses was instructed in all the wisdom of the Egyptians, and he was mighty in his words and deeds. [23] "When he was forty years old, it came into his heart to visit his brethren, the sons of Israel. [24] And seeing one of them being wronged, he defended the oppressed man and avenged him by striking the Egyptian. [25] He supposed that his brethren understood that God was giving them deliverance by his hand, but they did not understand. [26] And on the following day he appeared to them as they were quarreling and would have reconciled them, saying, 'Men, you are brethren, why do you wrong each other?' [27] But the man who was wronging his neighbor thrust him aside, saying, 'Who made you a ruler and a judge over us? [28] Do you want to kill me as you killed the Egyptian yesterday?' [29] At this retort Moses fled, and became an exile in the land of Midian, where he became the father of two sons. [30] "Now when forty years had passed, an angel appeared to him in the

wilderness of Mount Sinai, in a flame of fire in a bush. [31] When Moses saw it he wondered at the sight; and as he drew near to look, the voice of the Lord came, [32] 'I am the God of your fathers, the God of Abraham and of Isaac and of Jacob.' And Moses trembled and did not dare to look. [33] And the Lord said to him, 'Take off the shoes from your feet, for the place where you are standing is holy ground. [34] I have surely seen the ill-treatment of my people that are in Egypt and heard their groaning, and I have come down to deliver them. And now come, I will send you to Egypt.'

[35] "This Moses whom they refused, saying, 'Who made you a ruler and a judge?' God sent as both ruler and deliverer by the hand of the angel that appeared to him in the bush. [36] He led them out, having performed wonders and signs in Egypt and at the Red Sea, and in the wilderness for forty years. [37] This is the Moses who said to the Israelites, 'God will raise up for you a prophet from your brethren as he raised me up.' [38] This is he who was in the congregation in the wilderness with the angel who spoke to him at Mount Sinai, and with our fathers; and he received living oracles to give to us. [39] Our fathers refused to obey him, but thrust him aside, and in their hearts they turned to Egypt, [40] saying to Aaron, 'Make for us gods to go before us; as for this Moses who led us out from the land of Egypt, we do not know what has become of him.' [41] And they made a calf in those days, and offered a sacrifice to the idol and rejoiced in the works of their hands. [42] But God turned and gave them over to worship the host of heaven, as it is written in the book of the prophets: 'Did you offer to me slain beasts and sacrifices, forty years in the wilderness, O house of Israel? [43] And you took up the tent of Moloch, and the star of the god Rephan, the figures which you made to worship; and I will remove you beyond Babylon.' "

In his recounting of the story of the exodus, Stephen was careful to portray the strain that existed between Moses and the Israelites. Although Moses was God's prophet, the people rejected him because of their hard hearts. In the same way, the Jews of Stephen's day rejected Jesus, the prophet who Moses said would come after him (Acts 7:37; Deuteronomy 18:15-18). Filled with the Holy Spirit, Stephen himself was speaking prophetically, yet even as he spoke he realized that the hearts of his listeners were hardening and he too would probably be rejected.

As we read this story of Stephen, we need to be careful not to think that he was railing against all the Jews. Stephen himself was a Jew, although one born and bred in a more gentile-populated territory than Jerusalem. His example of the Israelites' response to prophets sent by God reflects the tension that exists between God and all people. Moved by the Holy Spirit, he was pointing to the stubbornness and hardness of heart toward God that is common to every race and nation. He was describing a conflict that exists because each one of us has had our relationship with God marred by sin.

Some of us seldom see the darkness in our hearts and feel perfectly justified in our positions. Others may walk around acutely aware of the inner strife but feel helpless to change. Many of us fall somewhere in between these two extremes. Wherever we are, God wants us to know that we can overcome our obstacles through a daily examination of conscience and repentance.

Can you identify the drives in you for self-centered living? Do you find it hard to trust in God's love and promises? What suspicions, prejudices, even resentments and hatreds, do you hold against other people? It's these sins—and others besides—that keep our hearts distant from God. It's because of these very sins that Jesus came and died for us in the first place.

We have great reason for hope. God has not abandoned us. We are in Christ. God has poured out his Spirit to form us and empower us and change us. Sin no longer has the power to keep us bound. Through Christ we can become loving, generous, and kind people in every aspect of our lives!

"Lord Jesus, I turn from sin and turn to you. Come into my heart more deeply and teach me to obey the Holy Spirit more fully. I place my faith in you. I believe that you can change me in an astounding way."

Acts 7:44-50

[44] "Our fathers had the tent of witness in the wilderness, even as he who spoke to Moses directed him to make it, according to the pattern that he had seen. [45] Our fathers in turn brought it in with Joshua when they dispossessed the nations which God thrust out before our fathers. So it was until the days of David, [46] who found favor in the sight of God and asked leave to find a habitation for the God of Jacob. [47] But it was Solomon who built a house for him. [48] Yet the Most High does not dwell in houses made with hands; as the prophet says, [49] 'Heaven is my throne, and earth my footstool. What house will you build for me, says the Lord, or what is the place of my rest? [50] Did not my hand make all these things?' " ✐

Stephen's bold and adventurous spirit propelled him forward in declaring the message of Jesus to the Jews. Like the great men who played a part in the history of Israel, he too was obedient to God's command and call on his life. When he was accused of speaking against and defaming the temple, he used Israel's own history to defend himself.

Stephen tried to show his listeners how they had slipped away from the truth that God is bigger than the temple; that heaven is his throne and earth is his footstool (Isaiah 66:1-2). They had come to esteem the temple and the practices that it stood for more than the God who dwelled in it. This kept many, though not all, from accepting the *living temple* in the person of Jesus Christ. As he defended himself, Stephen insisted that people had worshipped God long before there was a temple. God didn't dwell exclusively in places built by human hands. All of creation is his home.

Stephen's address to the Sanhedrin—indeed, his very life—shows how the Holy Spirit is always seeking to refine his people's understanding of God. Stephen had received the Spirit and allowed his life to be turned upside down because of it. A man of considerable talent, he became content to serve his fellow Christians, humbly waiting on tables and taking a position of lowliness. As a result of his openness to the Spirit, he became a vessel of grace for others as he preached the good news and did great signs and wonders among the people.

God is not confined to buildings. He dwells in anyone who praises and worships him with a humble and contrite heart. Of course, it is good to have a place that honors God and allows his people to gather in his name. But he is far too loving to limit himself to bricks and mortar. He wants to dwell in our hearts and minds in such a way that we are filled with the wonder and power of God. The more we come to know Jesus, the more joyful and confident we will become. Our hearts will be so filled that God's love will flow out to others and bring them blessing, healing, and comfort.

"Thank you, Lord Jesus, for the grace of your cross. Thank you for making me into a temple of the Holy Spirit. Help me to be courageous like Stephen in bringing the good news to the people with whom I live and work."

Acts 7:51–8:1

[51] "You stiff-necked people, uncircumcised in heart and ears, you always resist the Holy Spirit. As your fathers did, so do you. [52] Which of the prophets did not your fathers persecute? And they killed those who announced beforehand the coming of the Righteous One, whom you have now betrayed and murdered, [53] you who received the law as delivered by angels and did not keep it."

[54] Now when they heard these things they were enraged, and they ground their teeth against him. [55] But he, full of the Holy Spirit, gazed into heaven and saw the glory of God, and Jesus standing at the right hand of God; [56] and he said, "Behold, I see the heavens opened, and the Son of man standing at the right hand of God." [57] But they cried out with a loud voice and stopped their ears and rushed together upon him. [58] Then they cast him out of the city and stoned him; and the witnesses laid down their garments at the feet of a young man named Saul. [59] And as they were stoning Stephen, he prayed, "Lord Jesus, receive my spirit." [60] And he knelt down and cried with a loud voice, "Lord, do not hold this sin against them." And when he had said this, he fell asleep.

[1] And Saul was consenting to his death.

And on that day a great persecution arose against the church in Jerusalem; and they were all scattered throughout the region of Judea and Samaria, except the apostles.

Facing accusers who were already enraged and prepared to stone him, Stephen refused to back down. Instead, he called these elders "stiff-necked people, uncircumcised in heart and ears" and resistant to the Holy Spirit (Acts 7:51). Do we have the courage to stand fast before our accusers? Are we ready to die for our convictions about Jesus? Stephen continued to speak the words God gave him because he was compelled by the Holy Spirit. His life, in many ways, paralleled the life of Jesus; both were full of grace and able to bring about miracles.

What did Stephen mean when he described his accusers as "uncircumcised"? In the Book of Deuteronomy, Moses spoke of the true value of the physical circumcision that was part of the Israelites' heritage: "The Lord your God will *circumcise your heart* . . . so that you will love [him] with all your heart and with all your soul, that you may live" (Deuteronomy 30:6, emphasis added). Under the new covenant, inaugurated by Jesus' death and resurrection, our old hearts of stone can now be replaced by hearts of flesh (see Ezekiel 36:26). Stephen described the elders as uncircumcised in heart because they had closed themselves to God to the point that he could not move in them and warm them with his love. Because they preferred their own wisdom to God's wisdom, their ears were uncircumcised as well—closed to the word of God. Relying on their self-righteousness, they could not receive the grace of the Spirit. They opposed all those who might have led them to redemption. They simply were not open to the Lord.

Let us be like Stephen, boldly speaking up for the truth of the Lord Jesus. Like Stephen, let us forgive our accusers so that the life of Jesus may manifest itself in us. Let us not fear the cross of persecution, misunderstanding, or slander. Instead, let us embrace it with hope and joy. Perhaps we will be called upon to witness to Jesus as Stephen did. What joy can be ours if we allow the cross to do its work!

"Holy Spirit, I surrender all of my ways to you. Move in me with such great power that Jesus is glorified in me just as he was in Stephen."

The Gospel Goes Out

ACTS
8:2–12:23

Acts 8:2-8

[2] Devout men buried Stephen, and made great lamentation over him.
[3] But Saul was ravaging the church, and entering house after house, he dragged off men and women and committed them to prison.
[4] Now those who were scattered went about preaching the word.
[5] Philip went down to a city of Samaria, and proclaimed to them the Christ. [6] And the multitudes with one accord gave heed to what was said by Philip, when they heard him and saw the signs which he did.
[7] For unclean spirits came out of many who were possessed, crying with a loud voice; and many who were paralyzed or lame were healed.
[8] So there was much joy in that city.

Just before his ascension, Jesus promised his apostles that they would be his witnesses "in Jerusalem, in all Judea and Samaria, and to the ends of the earth" (Acts 1:8). Earlier, he had promised Peter that even the gates of hell could not prevail against the church (Matthew 16:18). As the Book of Acts unfolds, we see signs of these promises coming to fulfillment. While Saul's persecution may have appeared to endanger the church, in reality the church only stretched its borders to Samaria and beyond. Nothing could prevail against it as God's people proclaimed the gospel, ultimately to every corner of the earth.

How did the church grow? We can identify three elements. First, "those who were scattered went from place to place, proclaiming the word" (Acts 8:4). They didn't rely on special techniques or philosophies. They didn't try to convince people to "join up" by making the church seem other than what God had called it to be. Rather, with uncomplicated faith in God, they spoke about his promises in Scripture and told how they were being fulfilled.

Second, Philip "proclaimed the Messiah" (Acts 8:5). As Paul would write some years later, "We do not proclaim ourselves; we proclaim Jesus Christ as Lord" (2 Corinthians 4:5). The church spread because Jesus Christ, crucified and risen, was at the heart of this proclamation. Confident of Christ's desire to make himself known, the first Christians spoke of Jesus as a living person, their Lord and God whose love had transformed their hearts. And they invited their hearers to know this person as well.

Finally, those who heard Philip listened eagerly, "hearing and seeing the signs that he did" (Acts 8:6). Philip didn't just speak about Jesus. He demonstrated that Christ was real, that he was risen, and that his power and authority were absolute. Unclean spirits were cast out; the paralyzed were cured; the lame could walk. No one could deny that they were in the presence of something greater than human words and mortal ideas. They were faced with God's power, and they couldn't deny it.

What was true then is also true today. If we want to share the gospel with others and see the church grow, we too are called to trust in God's word, speak plainly about Jesus, and pray that his power will be demonstrated. Then we will see Jesus' promises for the church come to reality before our very eyes.

Acts 8:9-25

[9] But there was a man named Simon who had previously practiced magic in the city and amazed the nation of Samaria, saying that he himself was somebody great. [10] They all gave heed to him, from the least to the greatest, saying, "This man is that power of God which is called Great." [11] And they gave heed to him, because for a long time he had amazed them with his magic. [12] But when they believed Philip as he preached good news about the kingdom of God and the name of Jesus Christ, they were baptized, both men and women. [13] Even Simon

himself believed, and after being baptized he continued with Philip. And seeing signs and great miracles performed, he was amazed. [14] Now when the apostles at Jerusalem heard that Samaria had received the word of God, they sent to them Peter and John, [15] who came down and prayed for them that they might receive the Holy Spirit; [16] for it had not yet fallen on any of them, but they had only been baptized in the name of the Lord Jesus. [17] Then they laid their hands on them and they received the Holy Spirit. [18] Now when Simon saw that the Spirit was given through the laying on of the apostles' hands, he offered them money, [19] saying, "Give me also this power, that any one on whom I lay my hands may receive the Holy Spirit." [20] But Peter said to him, "Your silver perish with you, because you thought you could obtain the gift of God with money! [21] You have neither part nor lot in this matter, for your heart is not right before God. [22] Repent therefore of this wicked-ness of yours, and pray to the Lord that, if possible, the intent of your heart may be forgiven you. [23] For I see that you are in the gall of bitter-ness and in the bond of iniquity." [24] And Simon answered, "Pray for me to the Lord, that nothing of what you have said may come upon me." [25] Now when they had testified and spoken the word of the Lord, they returned to Jerusalem, preaching the gospel to many villages of the Samaritans.

Simon had quite a following in Samaria. Using occult powers, he was able to perform wonders that no ordinary person could do. As a result, people revered him and considered him someone to be respected and admired.

When Philip arrived, everything changed. Philip didn't have the power of occult magic, he had the "super-power" of the gospel, and he was simply overflowing with the love of Christ. Philip's miracles and his testimony about Jesus cut the Samaritans to their hearts and made them want to receive the life of Jesus for themselves. Even Simon was awed by what he saw.

This story raises two good questions for us to ask ourselves. First, how do I view Jesus? Do I view him as the Samaritans viewed Simon—just as someone to call on for a quick fix or a quick miracle to get me out of trouble? Or do I see him as the Son of God, who wants to come into my life and transform me with his power and love? Secondly, is my daily witness more like Philip's or more like Simon's? Do I try to attract or impress people by showing off my many talents and skills, or do I spend my energy obeying Jesus and simply letting his love shine from my heart? Christ in us is our one hope of glory.

There will always be individuals who rise to prominence and seem capable of captivating and impressing people. We may be struck by their wisdom, physical strength, athletic skill, or beauty. But the Lord wants to ask us: Will you allow yourself to be drawn to me? Will you allow me to shower my love and grace on you? Will you allow me to work powerful miracles of healing and forgiveness in you and through you? The world has enough impressive people. What it needs now is more people who shine forth with the light of Jesus. Do you believe you can be one of those people?

"Father, I want to live my life like Philip, not like Simon. Fill me with the light of Jesus and the power of the Holy Spirit. Make me more like you today, Lord, and may others be drawn to me because of your life in me."

Acts 8:26-40

26 But an angel of the Lord said to Philip, "Rise and go toward the south to the road that goes down from Jerusalem to Gaza." This is a desert road. 27 And he rose and went. And behold, an Ethiopian, a eunuch, a minister of Candace, queen of the Ethiopians, in charge of all her treasure, had

come to Jerusalem to worship [28] and was returning; seated in his chariot, he was reading the prophet Isaiah. [29] And the Spirit said to Philip, "Go up and join this chariot." [30] So Philip ran to him, and heard him reading Isaiah the prophet, and asked, "Do you understand what you are reading?" [31] And he said, "How can I, unless some one guides me?" And he invited Philip to come up and sit with him. [32] Now the passage of the scripture which he was reading was this: "As a sheep led to the slaughter or a lamb before its shearer is dumb, so he opens not his mouth. [33] In his humiliation justice was denied him. Who can describe his generation? For his life is taken up from the earth." [34] And the eunuch said to Philip, "About whom, pray, does the prophet say this, about himself or about some one else?" [35] Then Philip opened his mouth, and beginning with this scripture he told him the good news of Jesus. [36] And as they went along the road they came to some water, and the eunuch said, "See, here is water! What is to prevent my being baptized?" [38] And he commanded the chariot to stop, and they both went down into the water, Philip and the eunuch, and he baptized him. [39] And when they came up out of the water, the Spirit of the Lord caught up Philip; and the eunuch saw him no more, and went on his way rejoicing. [40] But Philip was found at Azotus, and passing on he preached the gospel to all the towns till he came to Caesarea. ✒

Chances are that we would not be Christians today if it were not for someone ministering to us as Philip ministered to the Ethiopian eunuch. Perhaps a parent, a friend, or even a perfect stranger was at the right place at the right time. They explained about Jesus just as our hearts were stirred by the Holy Spirit. And, like Philip, all of us can help bring Jesus to others. But how did Philip manage to work such miracles?

In the case of the Ethiopian, Philip obeyed God's command and headed right for the Gaza road. He did not wait for another sign to convince him. When he saw the Ethiopian's chariot, he did not hesitate at all. He ran up and sought to engage him in conversation. When he saw the man reading Scripture, Philip realized that God had been preparing the Ethiopian's heart: The eunuch already had many questions. All Philip had to do was obey God. As a result of such simple obedience, the Ethiopian wanted to be baptized into Christ right away.

We too are called to bring Jesus to those who have not heard or do not understand the gospel. In our families, among our friends, or even with acquaintances and strangers, we can become mighty instruments of God's grace. The key, as Philip demonstrated, is to be ready and willing to serve God. This is what becoming Christlike means. One of the most convincing witnesses to Christ for many people is the testimony of someone in their own circle who is surrendered to God. Like Philip, they are used by God because they have made themselves available to him. And then when the time comes, they simply obey the Holy Spirit.

God will always provide us with the tools necessary to bring others to Jesus. Would an all-good God send us out and not give us what we need? No. "We are his workmanship, created in Christ Jesus for good works, which God prepared beforehand" (Ephesians 2:10). Let us bring the miraculous power of God into every situation. We can bring healing, deliverance, reconciliation, and hope to everyone—even when, by human standards, situations may seem hopeless.

"Jesus, we praise you today. May we enter your courts with praise and gratitude as we help to bring your great mercy and faithfulness to all peoples."

Acts 9:1-9

[1] But Saul, still breathing threats and murder against the disciples of the Lord, went to the high priest [2] and asked him for letters to the synagogues at Damascus, so that if he found any belonging to the Way, men or women, he might bring them bound to Jerusalem. [3] Now as he journeyed he approached Damascus, and suddenly a light from heaven flashed about him. [4] And he fell to the ground and heard a voice saying to him, "Saul, Saul, why do you persecute me?" [5] And he said, "Who are you, Lord?" And he said, "I am Jesus, whom you are persecuting; [6] but rise and enter the city, and you will be told what you are to do." [7] The men who were traveling with him stood speechless, hearing the voice but seeing no one. [8] Saul arose from the ground; and when his eyes were opened, he could see nothing; so they led him by the hand and brought him into Damascus. [9] And for three days he was without sight, and neither ate nor drank.

God works in ways we do not expect. Saul was a brilliant young scholar (Galatians 1:14) who, enraged by the adherents of the Way (Acts 7:54,58), consented to Stephen's death (8:1) and embarked on a murderous persecution of the followers of Christ (9:1-2). Yet God called him to build the church he was trying to destroy. Once violently opposed to the gospel, Saul became one of its greatest proclaimers and champions. With God's powerful intervention, Saul's life underwent an extraordinary change. The early Christians were astounded: "Is not this the man who made havoc in Jerusalem?" (9:21). Clearly, the conversion of Saul was something quite unexpected!

God can work in any way he wants. He lacks neither power, authority, nor will to accomplish his intention. He demonstrated this dramatically—not only in Saul's life but repeatedly throughout the history of salvation. Who would expect that Moses—raised as an Egyptian prince—would be called by God to lead the Hebrews to the Promised Land? Or that David—a shepherd and the youngest son of Jesse—would become the greatest king of Israel, from whose line the Savior of the world descended? Or that Esther, Jewish exile, having won the Persian king's favor, would be the instrument to save her fellow Jews from annihilation? Consider God's call to Mary to be the mother of Jesus, or to the fisherman Peter and the tax collector Levi to be apostles. God called; they responded; and those around them could not stand in the way.

Nothing is an insurmountable obstacle to God—neither disability, nor social standing, hostile disposition, nor any circumstance of life. God's power transcends and can transform all things into opportunities to advance the gospel. The only impediment is our free will, which God will not force. Ananias initially objected to God's choice of Saul, then submitted to it. Through his prayers, Saul was baptized and filled with the Holy Spirit (Acts 9:17-18).

Let's examine our own lives: Do we stand in the way of God's work in us or in others because it doesn't fit with our preconceptions of what God should do? God *can* call and *has* called people who seem unlikely candidates to do his work—Francis of Assisi, Rose of Lima, and John Vianney to name a few. St. Paul was among the first of these, but the call to conversion and to witness still sounds among us. Let us not restrict God's call and God's work by our own ideas.

Acts 9:10-19

[10] Now there was a disciple at Damascus named Ananias. The Lord said to him in a vision, "Ananias." And he said, "Here I am, Lord." [11] And the Lord said to him, "Rise and go to the street called Straight, and inquire in the house of Judas for a man of Tarsus named Saul; for behold, he is praying, [12] and he has seen a man named Ananias come in and lay his hands on him so that he might regain his sight." [13] But Ananias answered, "Lord, I have heard from many about this man, how much evil he has done to thy saints at Jerusalem; [14] and here he has authority from the chief priests to bind all who call upon thy name." [15] But the Lord said to him, "Go, for he is a chosen instrument of mine to carry my name before the Gentiles and kings and the sons of Israel; [16] for I will show him how much he must suffer for the sake of my name." [17] So Ananias departed and entered the house. And laying his hands on him he said, "Brother Saul, the Lord Jesus who appeared to you on the road by which you came, has sent me that you may regain your sight and be filled with the Holy Spirit." [18] And immediately something like scales fell from his eyes and he regained his sight. Then he rose and was baptized, [19] and took food and was strengthened.

Ananias was the right man in the right place at the right time. But he still must have wondered to himself if he was understanding correctly. We can almost hear him as he protested to Jesus: "Lord, I know you died and rose from the dead and are filled with all knowledge. . . . But are you sure that this Saul is the man? We've all heard about him and what he's been doing in Jerusalem and why he came to Damascus!"

Ananias couldn't see then that God was going to use Saul in a powerful way to build the church of Jesus Christ. "Go, for he is a chosen instrument of mine to carry my name before the Gentiles and kings and sons of Israel" (Acts 9:15). The Lord could never convince Ananias of this on logical grounds. After all, who could conceive of such a tormentor being used to proclaim the gospel and to build up the body of Christ? Eventually, Ananias realized that he had to listen. He was obedient to God, despite the personal risk, because he trusted God and had to act accordingly (9:17).

Through his obedience to God, Ananias became Saul's link to the church; his change of heart was so complete that he even addressed Saul as "brother" (Acts 9:17). Through Ananias, Saul began to experience the life and energy of Christian community. He would learn what it meant to live with other believers and receive teaching that would bear fruit in his life (9:19-25).

God works in the lives of ordinary people to carry out his plans. We should not regard this story as just a curious event from biblical times. God wants us to understand that he can work in our lives, just as he has worked in the lives of countless men and women throughout salvation history. The Lord needs all of us to do his work. Think how differently things might have gone if Ananias—from fear or bitterness—had disobeyed God.

"Lord Jesus, I want to be used by you to build your kingdom. Through the Holy Spirit, teach me the truths of the kingdom of God and enable me to serve you through the power of your death and resurrection. I embrace your call and blessing."

Acts 9:19-30

[19] For several days he was with the disciples at Damascus. [20] And in the synagogues immediately he proclaimed Jesus, saying, "He is the Son of God." [21] And all who heard him were amazed, and said, "Is not this the man who made havoc in Jerusalem of those who called on this name? And he has come here for this purpose, to bring them bound before the chief priests." [22] But Saul increased all the more in strength, and confounded the Jews who lived in Damascus by proving that Jesus was the Christ.

[23] When many days had passed, the Jews plotted to kill him, [24] but their plot became known to Saul. They were watching the gates day and night, to kill him; [25] but his disciples took him by night and let him down over the wall, lowering him in a basket.

[26] And when he had come to Jerusalem he attempted to join the disciples; and they were all afraid of him, for they did not believe that he was a disciple. [27] But Barnabas took him, and brought him to the apostles, and declared to them how on the road he had seen the Lord, who spoke to him, and how at Damascus he had preached boldly in the name of Jesus. [28] So he went in and out among them at Jerusalem, [29] preaching boldly in the name of the Lord. And he spoke and disputed against the Hellenists; but they were seeking to kill him. [30] And when the brethren knew it, they brought him down to Caesarea, and sent him off to Tarsus.

I magine if Yasser Arafat suddenly announced he had converted to Judaism. What kind of reaction do you think such news would provoke among the Israelis? Would they trust him? This can give us some sense of how the elders of the church in Jerusalem first approached Saul. A prominent Pharisee, he had turned from persecuting Christians to proclaiming that Jesus really was the Son of God. This was very impressive indeed, but the apostles wanted to set Saul on firmer footing before they let him witness in the name of the church.

Saul certainly did have a lot to learn! It seems that no matter where he went, he got himself, and even the church, into trouble. Of course, we should give him credit for courageously standing up for his newfound faith. But at the same time, Saul was just beginning his walk with the Lord, and there were many rough edges that needed to be smoothed out. Therefore the elders sent Saul away to Tarsus so that he could sit quietly, ponder Scripture, and draw close to Jesus in his heart.

Jesus Christ, the head of the church, sees a vast amount of potential in each one of us. We are all indispensable! In fulfillment of the prophecy of Joel that Peter quoted on Pentecost Sunday (Joel 2:28-32; Acts 2:17-21), God truly has poured out his Spirit. Throughout the ages men and women have seen visions, dreamed dreams, and heard the voice of the Lord.

Our lives may not be as dramatic as Saul's or those of other great saints, but the promises are the same for everyone who freely chooses to receive and cooperate with grace. Saul didn't become St. Paul because he was a good person. It happened because he persevered in prayer and kept surrendering his heart to Jesus.

Persevering in prayer as Saul did during his years in Tarsus can prepare us to fulfill our potential as fruitful imitators of Christ. As we persist, we will discover that we can live sacrificial lives, conformed not to this world but to Christ. More than anything else, our goal should be to become like Jesus—to let his heart of love and compassion transform us so that we can love as he loves. Just as it took Saul years to become the great St. Paul, so it will take us time. The more we persist, the greater the result will become.

"Jesus, how vital it is to sit, to listen, and to learn from you! How necessary it is to receive your love which surpasses all knowledge. If I had all knowledge but had not your love, I would be nothing. Help me to stay close to you and to be patient. I trust that you will transform me."

Acts 9:31-43

³¹ So the church throughout all Judea and Galilee and Samaria had peace and was built up; and walking in the fear of the Lord and in the comfort of the Holy Spirit it was multiplied.

³² Now as Peter went here and there among them all, he came down also to the saints that lived at Lydda. ³³ There he found a man named Aeneas, who had been bedridden for eight years and was paralyzed. ³⁴ And Peter said to him, "Aeneas, Jesus Christ heals you; rise and make your bed." And immediately he rose. ³⁵ And all the residents of Lydda and Sharon saw him, and they turned to the Lord.

³⁶ Now there was at Joppa a disciple named Tabitha, which means Dorcas. She was full of good works and acts of charity. ³⁷ In those days she fell sick and died; and when they had washed her, they laid her in an upper room. ³⁸ Since Lydda was near Joppa, the disciples, hearing that Peter was there, sent two men to him entreating him, "Please come to us without delay." ³⁹ So Peter rose and went with them. And when he had come, they took him to the upper room. All the widows stood beside him weeping, and showing tunics and other garments which Dorcas made while she was with them. ⁴⁰ But Peter put them all outside and knelt down and prayed; then turning to the body he said, "Tabitha, rise." And she opened her eyes, and when she saw Peter she sat up. ⁴¹ And he gave her his hand and lifted her up. Then calling the saints and widows he presented her alive. ⁴² And it became known throughout all Joppa, and many believed in the Lord. ⁴³ And he stayed in Joppa for many days with one Simon, a tanner.

The miracles of God are meant to be more than just spectacular displays of power; they are intended to touch us personally with the love of God. In fact, the Book of Acts gives the impression that miracles can be part of our daily lives—and that their effects can reach into our homes, businesses, and communities. Throughout Luke's collection of stories of life in the early Christian community, we see the first believers very simply including God in their daily walk.

Aeneas' healing and Tabitha's recall from the dead were miraculous events, yet Peter simply told Aeneas, "Jesus Christ heals you; rise and make your bed" (Acts 9:34). He spoke so casually, as though it was nothing remarkable! Similarly, Tabitha's friends had begged Peter to come after she died. When he arrived, all he said was, "Tabitha, rise" (9:40). Then he went off to see a friend. Peter—and presumably the whole community—seemed to be accustomed to seeing God work in their midst. Luke's point was to present these miracles in the context of *ordinary living*.

The people of the new church undoubtedly were touched and came to a deeper belief in the Lord through these events, but the miracles involved the cares and concerns of daily life. The apostles were simply following in Jesus' footsteps. Jesus told them that they could feed the hungry, heal the sick, cast out demons, and calm the storms. They believed, and sought to live in the light of his promises. Knowing this, why do we hesitate to involve the Lord in the practical matters of *our* daily lives?

The same Jesus who healed Aeneas and who raised Tabitha from the dead is living and active today. As followers of Jesus, we too are called to walk in the same ways that the saints and apostles did: proclaiming freedom to the captives, healing for the sick, and life to the dead. Miraculous things can still occur on a daily basis. We need only ask in faith.

"Heavenly Father, give us humble, teachable hearts. We know that your works through us don't depend on us one-tenth as much as they depend on you. Encourage us as we launch out to do the work of your kingdom. Let your works become part of our daily lives."

Acts 10:1-8

[1] At Caesarea there was a man named Cornelius, a centurion of what was known as the Italian Cohort, [2] a devout man who feared God with all his household, gave alms liberally to the people, and prayed constantly to God. [3] About the ninth hour of the day he saw clearly in a vision an angel of God coming in and saying to him, "Cornelius." [4] And he stared at him in terror, and said, "What is it, Lord?" And he said to him, "Your prayers and your alms have ascended as a memorial before God. [5] And now send men to Joppa, and bring one Simon who is called Peter; [6] he is lodging with Simon, a tanner, whose house is by the seaside." [7] When the angel who spoke to him had departed, he called two of his servants and a devout soldier from among those that waited on him, [8] and having related everything to them, he sent them to Joppa.

The story of the conversion of Cornelius and his household marks a pivotal point in the Book of Acts and in the history of the early church. God's promises are extended beyond the Jews, and Jesus indeed becomes "a light for revelation to the Gentiles" (Luke 2:32) Centuries earlier, God foretold, "I will pour out my Spirit upon all flesh" (Joel 2:28). Now, we see him setting in motion something that will radically change the course of history. Christianity is about to extend beyond Judaism and establish a universal identity.

The setting for this event is Caesarea, a port city built by Herod the Great on the Mediterranean coast. One of the chief players is Cornelius, a centurion of the Roman cohort stationed there. Though a Gentile—an "alien" considered by the Jews to be outside the promises of God—Cornelius embraced the one God of Israel and was very generous to the Jewish people. He was not a full convert to Judaism (he was not circumcised and did not adhere to all the observances of the Mosaic law), but he was a devout man. In fact, it was as Cornelius was keeping one of the traditional times of worship in the Jewish liturgy that God spoke to him.

As important a role as Cornelius was to play in the coming drama, an even greater role was played by the director, God himself. It was God who instructed Cornelius to send for Simon Peter, and as we will see, it is God who convinces Peter to take the fateful step of entering the home of a Gentile—something a faithful Jew would never do. As the story unfolds, we'll also see that it is only through the work of God that the Christians in Jerusalem will be able to accept the startling revelation that salvation was available to Gentiles just as freely as it was available to Jews.

God is dedicated to his purposes. No one is excluded from his love and grace. How encouraging this can be for us! If God would take the initiative with Cornelius, why would he not take the initiative with us? Jesus came to give everyone life to the full. Confident of his love, let's be bold in our intercession, certain that God cares for us and for all people.

"Lord, your love knows no boundaries! Your generosity has no limits! Thank you for offering the gift of salvation and your Spirit to every man and woman you have ever created."

Acts 10:9-23

[9] The next day, as they were on their journey and coming near the city, Peter went up on the housetop to pray, about the sixth hour.
[10] And he became hungry and desired something to eat; but while they were preparing it, he fell into a trance [11] and saw the heaven opened, and something descending, like a great sheet, let down by four corners upon the earth. [12] In it were all kinds of animals and reptiles and birds of the air. [13] And there came a voice to him, "Rise, Peter; kill and eat." [14] But Peter said, "No, Lord; for I have never eaten anything that is common or unclean." [15] And the voice came to him again a second time, "What God has cleansed, you must not call common." [16] This happened three times, and the thing was taken up at once to heaven. [17] Now while Peter was inwardly perplexed as to what the vision which he had seen might mean, behold, the men that were sent by Cornelius, having made inquiry for Simon's house, stood before the gate [18] and called out to ask whether Simon who was called Peter was lodging there. [19] And while Peter was pondering the vision, the Spirit said to him, "Behold, three men are looking for you. [20] Rise and go down, and accompany them without hesitation; for I have sent them." [21] And Peter went down to the men and said, "I am the one you are looking for; what is the reason for your coming?" [22] And they said, "Cornelius, a centurion, an upright and God-fearing man, who is well spoken of by the whole Jewish nation, was directed by a holy angel to send for you to come to his house, and to hear what you have to say." [23] So he called them in to be his guests. The next day he rose and went off with them, and some of the brethren from Joppa accompanied him.

It was simply unthinkable to Peter to eat foods that Jewish tradition said were unclean. It was even more unthinkable to eat those foods with Gentiles. God's chosen people were called to separate themselves from the corrupt pagan nations around them. That was as it had always been. Now that God had acted so boldly in his life through Jesus, wouldn't Peter want to strive to keep the law of Moses even more perfectly?

Yet the Holy Spirit was working to expand Peter's vision. Because he wanted to help Peter make such a radical departure from his former ideas, God gave him a vision of heaven with a message he repeated three times—just to make sure he understood (Acts 10:16)!

In his natural mind, Peter recoiled at the idea of violating the kosher laws of his people, but in his heart he heard the Holy Spirit say, "What God has cleansed, you must not call common" (Acts 10:15). Peter pondered these words with an open mind and soon came to understand their meaning. God had not only cleansed the Jews to receive the Holy Spirit, but the Gentiles as well.

God's deepest desire is to cleanse and purify every human being and to fill them with the divine life of the Holy Spirit. Our Father looks upon all of us and says we are "very good" (Genesis 1:31). None of us is too sinful for Jesus to accept. None of us is so unclean that he simply won't even try to touch our hearts. Just as Peter had to learn to accept Gentiles as brothers and sisters, so God wants us to learn to accept everybody as equal heirs of his kingdom. There's no difference in his eyes, and he wants us to have the same attitude.

Let us examine our hearts and ask the Spirit to reveal any prejudices that might be lurking inside. We may have racial prejudices, or even denominational prejudices that interfere with the Holy Spirit's work of unifying Christians of different traditions. Like Peter, we can cooperate with the Holy Spirit and remain open to whatever he wants to do— even if it shatters our own preconceived notions of how God wants to act in the world.

"Holy Spirit, soften my heart and give me the grace to reach out to those who might feel unacceptable or unclean. Teach me to be open and to cooperate with your plan for building up the kingdom of God."

Acts 10:24-48

[24] And on the following day they entered Caesarea. Cornelius was expecting them and had called together his kinsmen and close friends. [25] When Peter entered, Cornelius met him and fell down at his feet and worshiped him. [26] But Peter lifted him up, saying, "Stand up; I too am a man." [27] And as he talked with him, he went in and found many persons gathered; [28] and he said to them, "You yourselves know how unlawful it is for a Jew to associate with or to visit any one of another nation; but God has shown me that I should not call any man common or unclean. [29] So when I was sent for, I came without objection. I ask then why you sent for me."

[30] And Cornelius said, "Four days ago, about this hour, I was keeping the ninth hour of prayer in my house; and behold, a man stood before me in bright apparel, [31] saying, 'Cornelius, your prayer has been heard and your alms have been remembered before God. [32] Send therefore to Joppa and ask for Simon who is called Peter; he is lodging in the house of Simon, a tanner, by the seaside.' [33] So I sent to you at once, and you have been kind enough to come. Now therefore we are all here present in the sight of God, to hear all that you have been commanded by the Lord."

[34] And Peter opened his mouth and said: "Truly I perceive that God shows no partiality, [35] but in every nation any one who fears him and does what is right is acceptable to him. [36] You know the word which he sent to Israel, preaching good news of peace by Jesus Christ (he is Lord of all), [37] the word which was proclaimed throughout all Judea, beginning from Galilee after the baptism which John preached: [38] how God

anointed Jesus of Nazareth with the Holy Spirit and with power; how he went about doing good and healing all that were oppressed by the devil, for God was with him. [39] And we are witnesses to all that he did both in the country of the Jews and in Jerusalem. They put him to death by hanging him on a tree; [40] but God raised him on the third day and made him manifest; [41] not to all the people but to us who were chosen by God as witnesses, who ate and drank with him after he rose from the dead. [42] And he commanded us to preach to the people, and to testify that he is the one ordained by God to be judge of the living and the dead. [43] To him all the prophets bear witness that every one who believes in him receives forgiveness of sins through his name."
[44] While Peter was still saying this, the Holy Spirit fell on all who heard the word. [45] And the believers from among the circumcised who came with Peter were amazed, because the gift of the Holy Spirit had been poured out even on the Gentiles. [46] For they heard them speaking in tongues and extolling God. Then Peter declared, [47] "Can any one forbid water for baptizing these people who have received the Holy Spirit just as we have?" [48] And he commanded them to be baptized in the name of Jesus Christ. Then they asked him to remain for some days. ✒

Commentators have likened the Acts of the Apostles to a play whose main character, the Holy Spirit, remains off-stage for much of the action. Waiting "in the wings," the Spirit nevertheless has a major role in guiding the events that shaped the early church and human history. Nowhere is this interaction more evident than during Peter's visit to the household of Cornelius.

This encounter could not have taken place without the Spirit's intervention just a few days earlier. Peter explained that fact to his hosts upon entering the Roman centurion's house: "You yourselves know how unlawful it is for a Jew to associate with or to visit any one of another nation" (Acts 10:28).

Yet Peter overcame this age-old taboo only because the Holy Spirit had shown him through a vision that he "should not call any man common or unclean" (Acts 10:28). Peter had opened his heart to that radical revelation, and as a result, accepted the Gentile's invitation. He went to Cornelius' house and began to share the good news with everyone there.

No one could have expected what happened next that day. Even Luke described the action as if the Spirit were an overenthusiastic actor unable to wait for his cue any longer. "While Peter was still saying this, the Holy Spirit fell on all who heard the word" (Acts 10:44).

God is always eager to enter and transform the lives of his children. Our God is not stingy with his love. He issues call after call, seeking sinners humble enough to admit their mistakes and turn back to him. How much more, for all who try sincerely to follow the Lord, should they expect that he can transform them into witnesses of his power to save.

Can you believe today that the Holy Spirit wants to enter your life just as mightily as he fell upon the believers in Caesarea? God's promise is that if you are fervent in prayer and open to his word like Peter and Cornelius, you too can experience a similar transformation of joy. For every step you take toward God, he is ready and willing to forge a deeper communion with you.

"Spirit of God, penetrate my heart more deeply, that I may proclaim my joy at your indwelling presence."

Acts 11:1-18

[1] Now the apostles and the brethren who were in Judea heard that the Gentiles also had received the word of God. [2] So when Peter went up to Jerusalem, the circumcision party criticized him, [3] saying, "Why did you go to uncircumcised men and eat with them?" [4] But Peter began and explained to them in order: [5] "I was in the city of Joppa praying; and in a trance I saw a vision, something descending, like a great sheet, let down from heaven by four corners; and it came down to me. [6] Looking at it closely I observed animals and beasts of prey and reptiles and birds of the air. [7] And I heard a voice saying to me, 'Rise, Peter; kill and eat.' [8] But I said, 'No, Lord; for nothing common or unclean has ever entered my mouth.' [9] But the voice answered a second time from heaven, 'What God has cleansed you must not call common.' [10] This happened three times, and all was drawn up again into heaven. [11] At that very moment three men arrived at the house in which we were, sent to me from Caesarea. [12] And the Spirit told me to go with them, making no distinction. These six brethren also accompanied me, and we entered the man's house. [13] And he told us how he had seen the angel standing in his house and saying, 'Send to Joppa and bring Simon called Peter; [14] he will declare to you a message by which you will be saved, you and all your household.' [15] As I began to speak, the Holy Spirit fell on them just as on us at the beginning. [16] And I remembered the word of the Lord, how he said, 'John baptized with water, but you shall be baptized with the Holy Spirit.' [17] If then God gave the same gift to them as he gave to us when we believed in the Lord Jesus Christ, who was I that I could withstand God?" [18] When they heard this they were silenced. And they glorified God, saying, "Then to the Gentiles also God has granted repentance unto life."

Peter's reception of Cornelius and his household—all of them Gentiles—into the church caused a major dispute among the Christians in Jerusalem. When Peter returned to Jerusalem, he was criticized by the "circumcision party" for visiting these Gentiles and sharing table fellowship with them. The Jewish Christians wanted to be faithful to the traditions handed down by Moses, and eating with Gentiles was forbidden since it made one ritually unclean.

In one sense, we can understand why Peter's unorthodox move would upset these people's sensibilities. After all, Jesus himself was circumcised and lived according to the Law of Moses. What gave Peter— or anyone else, for that matter—the authority to disregard the law? Shouldn't these Gentiles be required to convert to Judaism first and then receive baptism?

By recounting the supernatural way that God had led him to Cornelius, Peter was able to bring peace to the situation and convince his accusers that this was God's doing, and not just a radical idea of his. Peter's vision in Joppa and the Holy Spirit's dramatic outpouring upon the Gentiles demonstrated God's initiative to bring Gentile and Jew together as equal partners in God's plan of salvation. What a remarkable revelation of God's mercy and love! No individual, no race, no class, no party is to be excluded from the Father's loving embrace!

What about you? Do you sometimes make snap judgments when you hear about something unusual happening in your church or your neighborhood? Do you take time to examine your heart to make sure you're not being affected by prejudice or misunderstanding? Do you examine the situation carefully?

Who would have predicted the surprises of the Holy Spirit that we have witnessed in our age? Vatican II was a breath of fresh air for the renewal of the church. Pope John Paul II's inauguration of a new age of evangelization, the response of countless young people to be lights of hope for the new millennium, the work of ecumenism for breaking down old divisions and building unity, and the efforts of the pope to ask the Jewish people for forgiveness of past wrongs—all these are signs of God's action today in the church. God cannot be contained. He is ever on the move to change hearts, heal old wounds, and bring his kingdom to every corner of the world. Let's be receptive to the work and action of the Holy Spirit today.

"Holy Spirit, come and make my heart open and docile to your work of grace and renewal in my life, in the church, and in the world."

Acts 11:19-26

[19] Now those who were scattered because of the persecution that arose over Stephen traveled as far as Phoenicia and Cyprus and Antioch, speaking the word to none except Jews. [20] But there were some of them, men of Cyprus and Cyrene, who on coming to Antioch spoke to the Greeks also, preaching the Lord Jesus. [21] And the hand of the Lord was with them, and a great number that believed turned to the Lord. [22] News of this came to the ears of the church in Jerusalem, and they sent Barnabas to Antioch. [23] When he came and saw the grace of God, he was glad; and he exhorted them all to remain faithful to the Lord with steadfast purpose; [24] for he was a good man, full of the Holy Spirit and of faith. And a large company was added to the Lord. [25] So Barnabas went to Tarsus to look for Saul; [26] and when he had found him, he brought him to Antioch. For a whole year they met with the church, and taught a large company of people; and in Antioch the disciples were for the first time called Christians.

After interrupting his account of the church's spread from Jerusalem out to the broader world, Luke returns to those who were scattered from the holy city because of Stephen's martyrdom (Acts 11:19; 8:1,4). Again we see the wisdom of God, in that the martyrdom of one servant led to the spread of the gospel along the Mediterranean coast as far as Antioch, a major city with a sizable Jewish population.

The pattern up to this point was for those dispersed to speak only to Jews—either Palestinian or Hellenistic—about the gospel. Yet as the message spread farther afield, those who were converted began reaching out to the Gentiles as well. This led to the existence in Antioch of a new kind of church: part Jewish and part Greek, all Christian. Hearing about this new church, the apostles sent Barnabas to encourage them and to ensure that they were living according to the truth of the gospel. Barnabas was so impressed by what he saw that he decided to stay and continue to help them. To aid him in this work, he went to Tarsus to enlist Saul, who had withdrawn to pray and deepen his faith (Acts 11:22-26; Galatians 1:15-17).

Antioch was a marvel, for the unthinkable was happening: Jews and Gentiles were living together. Ancient divisions had given way to the "new creation" that Jesus came to inaugurate (Galatians 6:15). So distinctive and encompassing was their identity in Christ that these believers took on a new name: Christians, or "Christ-people." They weren't just adherents of a new philosophy; they were *united* with Jesus through baptism into his death and resurrection, and this union in Christ so changed them that a new name seemed appropriate.

In our age, at the beginning of a new century, we should ask ourselves: Do I know in my heart that I belong to Christ? Can I point to ways that union with him has changed me? Do I know victory over sin? Healing in relationships? Compassion for the burdened? A desire to serve God's people? These are all part of our inheritance as Christ's people, and they are available to everyone who turns to him in repentance and faith.

"Lord, we want to embrace our inheritance as your sons and daughters. Fill our hearts with confidence in your desire to make us all into a new creation. Teach us what it means to be your people."

Acts 11:27-30

²⁷ Now in these days prophets came down from Jerusalem to Antioch. ²⁸ And one of them named Agabus stood up and foretold by the Spirit that there would be a great famine over all the world; and this took place in the days of Claudius. ²⁹ And the disciples determined, every one according to his ability, to send relief to the brethren who lived in Judea; ³⁰ and they did so, sending it to the elders by the hand of Barnabas and Saul.

J erusalem was the center of the early church. However, because of the persecution that broke out over the martyrdom of Stephen, many Christians fled Jerusalem and settled in towns throughout the Roman Empire. As a result, the gospel of Jesus was preached in synagogues everywhere, but Jerusalem retained its position as "mother church."

It was up to the elders who remained in Jerusalem to consent to the baptizing of the Gentiles, initially through St. Peter and then others as they were dispersed throughout the empire. It was the elders in Jerusalem who sent Barnabas to investigate the effects of the gentile converts on the community of believers in Antioch. In many ways, Jerusalem held a special place in the hearts of the first Christians. Not only was it the place where Jesus died, it was also the place where the church was born.

When Agabus, a prophet who was a member of the church in Jerusalem, came to Antioch and predicted that a severe famine would strike the world, the believers took his words to heart. They decided to take up a collection from all the scattered churches and send the money to Jerusalem, where the need would be greatest. Even Paul, who was still held suspect by many in Jerusalem, volunteered to deliver the gifts there himself.

Heeding the cry of the poor has always been part of God's commands. The gospel of salvation in Jesus is meant to bring changes to our hearts and our actions. It's meant to fill us with the compassion of God and to impel us to go out in the world and make a difference, just as the first believers did. We cannot remain selfish. Jesus has a special love for the poor. Let us open our hearts to those in need around us. When we suffer with others, we suffer with Jesus. When we minister to them, we minister to Jesus. We can be sure that Jesus' comforting presence will overflow through us to those whom we serve.

"Jesus, I lift up to you all the people who are suffering from poverty or sickness. Show me how I can care for and encourage the needy in my neighborhood, even as I pray and intercede for all my poverty-stricken brothers and sisters around the world."

Acts 12:1-11

[1] About that time Herod the king laid violent hands upon some who belonged to the church. [2] He killed James the brother of John with the sword; [3] and when he saw that it pleased the Jews, he proceeded to arrest Peter also. This was during the days of Unleavened Bread. [4] And when he had seized him, he put him in prison, and delivered him to four squads of soldiers to guard him, intending after the Passover to bring him out to the people. [5] So Peter was kept in prison; but earnest prayer for him was made to God by the church.

[6] The very night when Herod was about to bring him out, Peter was sleeping between two soldiers, bound with two chains, and sentries

before the door were guarding the prison; [7] and behold, an angel of the Lord appeared, and a light shone in the cell; and he struck Peter on the side and woke him, saying, "Get up quickly." And the chains fell off his hands. [8] And the angel said to him, "Dress yourself and put on your sandals." And he did so. And he said to him, "Wrap your mantle around you and follow me." [9] And he went out and followed him; he did not know that what was done by the angel was real, but thought he was seeing a vision. [10] When they had passed the first and the second guard, they came to the iron gate leading into the city. It opened to them of its own accord, and they went out and passed on through one street; and immediately the angel left him. [11] And Peter came to himself, and said, "Now I am sure that the Lord has sent his angel and rescued me from the hand of Herod and from all that the Jewish people were expecting." ✒

Scripture talks about Peter's character and actions before Pentecost. Even though he had a very generous heart, he was restless, impetuous, temperamental, and even subject to fear.

A fisherman by trade, Peter was used to the sea, but on that day when a storm came up and the waves started tossing his boat about, he became very frightened (Matthew 14:24-32). Here was a circumstance over which he had no control, and he didn't know what to do. Peter often gave the impression that he was tough, but in denying the Lord three times, he showed how afraid and weak he really was (Luke 22:61). He was terrified of being arrested, tried, and perhaps even put to death because he was a follower of Jesus.

What changed Peter? How was he able to overcome his human frailties and lie sleeping so peacefully—chained between two guards, no less—awaiting his death? (Acts 12:6). On this night, even though Herod had just killed his fellow apostle James, Peter showed no signs of fear, no anger, no desire for revenge, and not a bit of restlessness. Such unlimited trust and faith as he exhibited could only exist in a true child of God.

Peter's transformation took place as he became aware of and learned to respond to the Holy Spirit in his life and as he witnessed the work of the Spirit in the church. The Spirit taught him to trust Jesus, no matter what situation he found himself in. He learned to take on the mind of Christ. No longer did his emotions, memories, or fears rule him. Jesus became his Lord, and gave Peter his peace. Fellowship with Jesus allowed Peter to take control over all his human weaknesses.

Like Peter, we too are called to a transformed life. We too are asked to entrust our lives to Jesus and to take all our thoughts captive to him. As we examine our hearts and acknowledge how far our minds are from the mind of God, we too can walk through this world as confidently and joyfully as Peter learned to do. We too can ask the Lord to teach us, direct our lives, and empower us to give glory to God the Father.

"Lord Jesus, I believe that your grace alone is sufficient to make me into as strong and faithful a believer as Peter. By your Spirit, teach me to surrender more to you."

Acts 12:12-23

[12] When he realized this, he went to the house of Mary, the mother of John whose other name was Mark, where many were gathered together and were praying. [13] And when he knocked at the door of the gateway, a maid named Rhoda came to answer. [14] Recognizing Peter's voice, in her joy she did not open the gate but ran in and told that Peter was standing at the gate. [15] They said to her, "You are mad." But she insisted that it was so. They said, "It is his angel!" [16] But Peter continued knocking; and when they opened, they saw him and were amazed. [17] But motioning to them with his hand to be silent, he

described to them how the Lord had brought him out of the prison. And he said, "Tell this to James and to the brethren." Then he departed and went to another place.

[18] Now when day came, there was no small stir among the soldiers over what had become of Peter. [19] And when Herod had sought for him and could not find him, he examined the sentries and ordered that they should be put to death. Then he went down from Judea to Caesarea, and remained there.

[20] Now Herod was angry with the people of Tyre and Sidon; and they came to him in a body, and having persuaded Blastus, the king's chamberlain, they asked for peace, because their country depended on the king's country for food. [21] On an appointed day Herod put on his royal robes, took his seat upon the throne, and made an oration to them. [22] And the people shouted, "The voice of a god, and not of man!" [23] Immediately an angel of the Lord smote him, because he did not give God the glory; and he was eaten by worms and died.

God's ways can seem so mysterious. Even Peter, when he was first set free from prison, thought he might be having a vision (Acts 12:9). But as soon as he realized what had happened, he blessed God and ran to tell the brothers and sisters. He experienced in a very real way the power of God and the power of intercessory prayer.

Herod, on the other hand, chose to find strength in himself and security in the power he had over people. He was never at rest. In the end, his desire for earthly power and security brought him down. Luke tells how Herod thought of himself as a god and even convinced many of his subjects to proclaim him as such. Such arrogance proved fatal.

How easy it is to leave prayer as the last resort! We can even somewhat enjoy the feeling we get when we allow worries to dominate our hearts and minds. We like to be in control of situations—even when they're just too big to handle alone and threaten to overwhelm us. To give our problems and concerns over to God, or to ask a brother or sister to pray with us is giving up some of that control. But God promises that if we do take steps like these, peace can replace anxiety, and freedom can replace the feeling of being tied up in knots. Even more importantly, Jesus himself will fill our hearts with love. He wants none of his children to feel bound by worry.

Sometimes we will lack the courage to place every situation in the Lord's hands. But each time we do open ourselves to a trusted brother or sister—each time we do surrender our fears and worries to the Lord—our faith is built up and we experience greater freedom. No matter how the situation ends up, shackles of fear lose their grip, and we grow in confidence and trust.

"Lord Jesus, I give you every difficult situation that I face—every single one. You know my fears. You know the ways I want to be in control. I choose instead to trust in you. You are my rock, and I know I will not be put to shame. You never abandon your children. Your ways are mysterious, but I still believe that you only want to do good for me and for all your people."

The First Organized Mission

ACTS
12:24–14:28

Acts 12:24–13:5

²⁴ But the word of God grew and multiplied. ²⁵ And Barnabas and Saul returned from Jerusalem when they had fulfilled their mission, bringing with them John whose other name was Mark.

¹ Now in the church at Antioch there were prophets and teachers, Barnabas, Simeon who was called Niger, Lucius of Cyrene, Mana-en a member of the court of Herod the tetrarch, and Saul. ² While they were worshiping the Lord and fasting, the Holy Spirit said, "Set apart for me Barnabas and Saul for the work to which I have called them." ³ Then after fasting and praying they laid their hands on them and sent them off. ⁴ So, being sent out by the Holy Spirit, they went down to Seleucia; and from there they sailed to Cyprus. ⁵ When they arrived at Salamis, they proclaimed the word of God in the synagogues of the Jews. And they had John to assist them. ✎

Despite the ferocity of the persecution that assailed the disciples of the infant church, "the word of God grew and multiplied" (Acts 12:24). Jesus had promises his disciples that they would receive power when the Holy Spirit came upon them and that they would be his witnesses to the ends of the earth (1:8). The account of the apostles' deeds, as described in the Acts of the Apostles, is like a "gospel of the Spirit." The Spirit was active in teaching, directing, and giving a prophetic word to the new church and so guiding it on its mission.

As they were fasting and praying together, the elders of the church at Antioch heard the Spirit tell them something new and different. They were to deputize some of their people as missionaries to spread the gospel. This was a new direction for the entire church. No longer would the elders simply hope and trust that the gospel would spread as people moved about. Now, the mandate to proclaim the gospel was much more purposeful. Imagine: Simply because these elders fasted and prayed, they were able to receive this new direction from the Spirit. But why during a fast? Why not just at any old time?

The Lord can *always* reach his people. However, sometimes we become preoccupied with our daily tasks and forget to open our hearts to the Spirit's gentle prompting. Fasting helps us to quiet our hearts and our minds. But what is considered to be a fast? Does it mean going without food? Sometimes it does mean that. But it can also be any number of other distraction-reducing, heart-quieting activities, like turning off the television or the car radio so that we can reflect on God's will for our lives.

It is important to remember that fasting should *always* be accompanied by prayer, as a way of giving our hearts to the Lord so that he can form us and empower us. Prayer and fasting help us to separate ourselves from our worldly thoughts and duties so that we can hear from God. As we quiet our hearts during a fast, we can come into God's presence more deeply and acknowledge who he is and who we are before him.

During our fasting and prayer, we are more open to hear the still, small voice of the Spirit. Perhaps he may open us up to a new and special work that he wants us to undertake. The Holy Spirit is still at work among God's people. As we quiet our souls and give the Lord more of our hearts, he will fill our lives with his gifts and fruit of the Spirit.

"Holy Spirit, you alone can guide us in the ways of God. We want to open ourselves to you so that the Father's plans can be accomplished through us. Give us the strength to fast—to quiet ourselves fully—so that we can be instruments of our Father's will."

Acts 13:6-12

⁶ When they had gone through the whole island as far as Paphos, they came upon a certain magician, a Jewish false prophet, named Bar-Jesus. ⁷ He was with the proconsul, Sergius Paulus, a man of intelligence, who summoned Barnabas and Saul and sought to hear the word of God. ⁸ But Elymas the magician (for that is the meaning of his name) withstood them, seeking to turn away the proconsul from the faith. ⁹ But Saul, who is also called Paul, filled with the Holy Spirit, looked intently at him ¹⁰ and said, "You son of the devil, you enemy of all righteousness, full of all deceit and villainy, will you not stop making crooked the straight paths of the Lord? ¹¹ And now, behold, the hand of the Lord is upon you, and you shall be blind and unable to see the sun for a time." Immediately mist and darkness fell upon him and he went about seeking people to lead him by the hand. ¹² Then the proconsul believed, when he saw what had occurred, for he was astonished at the teaching of the Lord. ✍

Having just been commissioned by the church in Antioch, Saul of Tarsus—now called Paul—began an exciting new phase in his life. Like Jesus after his baptism, empowerment by the Holy Spirit was followed immediately by a confrontation with the powers of darkness. How did Paul know that Elymas was a false prophet under the influence of the devil? What made Paul speak with such confidence and authority? Paul was filled with the Holy Spirit, and that Spirit enabled him to discern with God's wisdom, speak with God's authority, and enter into battle with God's power.

As he began his missionary work, Paul bore witness to the faithfulness of Jesus, who told the twelve not to worry about what they might face, "for the Holy Spirit will teach you in that very hour what you ought to say" (Luke 12:11-12). Jesus' promise was not just for the twelve apostles—Paul was not one of the original Twelve. In fact, he seems not to have had any personal contact with Jesus until the day he met him on the road to Damascus. Still, God empowered him just as much as Peter, James, and the rest. Paul's story here shows us that anyone united to God through baptism and faith in Jesus can stand up to the forces of darkness.

Satan is always ready to rob us of our joy and hope. When we encounter the forces of darkness that tempt us to believe that the situation we are praying about is hopeless, or when we are tempted to give in to worry and fear, we can stand strong in faith, inviting God's Spirit to fill us. All of us can take authority over darkness, call it what it really is, and cast it out in the name of Jesus.

Paul knew God's Spirit was one of power, love, and self-discipline (2 Timothy 1:7). Let us take the time to read the Father's word and allow the Spirit to reveal God's immense wisdom and love to us. Let's persist in spending time at the feet of the Lord, seeking to know him more clearly. Let's meditate on what he has done for us on the cross, especially how he has given us victory over the powers of darkness. As we stand against the powers of darkness, we can be assured that God will give us the victory!

"Holy Spirit, continue to fill me with your love in good measure, pressed down and running over, so it will flow from me to your world, dispelling the powers of darkness."

Acts 13:13-25

[13] Now Paul and his company set sail from Paphos, and came to Perga in Pamphylia. And John left them and returned to Jerusalem; [14] but they passed on from Perga and came to Antioch of Pisidia. And on the sabbath day they went into the synagogue and sat down. [15] After the reading of the law and the prophets, the rulers of the synagogue sent to them, saying, "Brethren, if you have any word of exhortation for the people, say it." [16] So Paul stood up, and motioning with his hand said: "Men of Israel, and you that fear God, listen. [17] The God of this people Israel chose our fathers and made the people great during their stay in the land of Egypt, and with uplifted arm he led them out of it. [18] And for about forty years he bore with them in the wilderness.

[19] And when he had destroyed seven nations in the land of Canaan, he gave them their land as an inheritance, for about four hundred and fifty years. [20] And after that he gave them judges until Samuel the prophet. [21] Then they asked for a king; and God gave them Saul the son of Kish, a man of the tribe of Benjamin, for forty years. [22] And when he had removed him, he raised up David to be their king; of whom he testified and said, 'I have found in David the son of Jesse a man after my heart, who will do all my will.' [23] Of this man's posterity God has brought to Israel a Savior, Jesus, as he promised. [24] Before his coming John had preached a baptism of repentance to all the people of Israel. [25] And as John was finishing his course, he said, 'What do you suppose that I am? I am not he. No, but after me one is coming, the sandals of whose feet I am not worthy to untie.' "

At the invitation of the rulers of the synagogue, Paul and Barnabas proclaimed the gospel of salvation to the people in Antioch of Pisidia. Paul began by reminding the people how God had delivered the Israelites from captivity in Egypt and brought them into the promised land. He then told them of God's faithfulness in providing judges and kings to rule and protect them. Finally he said that all of the promises of God have been fulfilled in Jesus Christ. "Of this man's posterity God has brought to Israel a Savior, Jesus, as he promised" (Acts 13:23). It is in Jesus Christ that our faith must rest.

The leaders of the early church continually preached the message of salvation through Jesus. They were tireless in their efforts to bring the good news to all, despite persecution, fatigue, hunger, deprivation, and ridicule. They were ordinary people, yet God transformed them. Their strength lay in the power of the death and resurrection of Christ and in the indwelling Holy Spirit.

We too can live new lives in Christ because of the Spirit dwelling in us. The Spirit gives us personal knowledge of Jesus, not just as a historical figure, but as an intimate, close companion. When we fully appreciate the privilege of knowing Jesus and his salvation, we can ignite in others a deep desire to know him too.

We sometimes think that the early disciples had an advantage over us because they were with Jesus in the flesh. In actuality, Jesus is present within us today even more vitally through the presence of the Holy Spirit in our hearts. After Pentecost, the disciples were transformed people because they knew that Jesus was in their midst in a way superior to that by which they knew him on earth.

"Lord Jesus, we ask you to convince us that we can be changed, as the early disciples were. Help us to know the power of your death and resurrection in our lives so that we can bring the gospel of salvation to others. We are your people; you are our God. Through your grace and mercy, we will be the people you call us to be."

Acts 13:26-43

26 "Brethren, sons of the family of Abraham, and those among you that fear God, to us has been sent the message of this salvation. 27 For those who live in Jerusalem and their rulers, because they did not recognize him nor understand the utterances of the prophets which are read every sabbath, fulfilled these by condemning him. 28 Though they could charge him with nothing deserving death, yet they asked Pilate to have him killed. 29 And when they had fulfilled all that was written of him, they took him down from the tree, and laid him in a tomb.

30 "But God raised him from the dead; 31 and for many days he appeared to those who came up with him from Galilee to Jerusalem, who are now his witnesses to the people. 32 And we bring you the good news that what God promised to the fathers, 33 this he has fulfilled to us their children by raising Jesus; as also it is written in the second psalm, 'Thou art my Son, today I have begotten thee.' 34 And as for the fact that he raised him from the dead, no more to return to corruption, he spoke in this way, 'I will give you the holy and sure blessings of David.' 35 Therefore he says also in another psalm, 'Thou wilt not let thy Holy One see corruption.'

36 For David, after he had served the counsel of God in his own generation, fell asleep, and was laid with his fathers, and saw corruption; 37 but he whom God raised up saw no corruption. 38 Let it be known to you therefore, brethren, that through this man forgiveness of sins is proclaimed to you, 39 and by him every one that believes is freed from everything from which you could not be freed by the law of Moses. 40 Beware, therefore, lest there come upon you what is said in the prophets: 41 'Behold, you scoffers, and wonder, and perish; for I do a deed in your days, a deed you will never believe, if one declares it to you.' "

42 As they went out, the people begged that these things might be told them the next sabbath. 43 And when the meeting of the synagogue broke up, many Jews and devout converts to Judaism followed Paul and Barnabas, who spoke to them and urged them to continue in the grace of God. ☙

Paul and Barnabas had been set apart and sent by the Holy Spirit to proclaim the word of God boldly to all who would listen (Acts 13:2). On their first missionary journey they traveled through the island of Cyprus and then into Asia Minor until they reached Antioch. Paul began his discourse to the Jews of Antioch by reminding them of God's faithfulness to Israel and of his promise to send a Savior, a promise that was fulfilled in Jesus. "We bring you the good news that what God promised to the fathers, this he has fulfilled to us their children by raising Jesus" (13:32-33).

In the early church, those who were filled with the Holy Spirit preached the good news of Jesus Christ. Peter, in his speech before the crowd gathered on Pentecost, preached the name, the works, the death, and resurrection of Jesus (Acts 2:22-23). Stephen, filled with the Holy Spirit, preached in this same way just before his death (7:2-53). These men were dramatically transformed by their encounter with Christ. The resurrection life of Christ had become their life. Paul, who previously had sought to destroy Christ's followers, was now boldly proclaiming salvation through Jesus.

It is important for us to reflect on this truth. Christ wants to change us just as he changed those in the early church. The grace of God is available if we earnestly desire the transforming power of the Lord. Every day we should ask Jesus to make us bold proclaimers of his gospel. The world today needs to hear the name of Jesus—that he is the Savior, the promised one. It needs to learn that through his obedience to the Father, all sin is forgiven. The world needs to hear that on the cross, death was defeated and eternal life was made possible.

The world around us is suffering for lack of knowledge of the truth of God. Let us who have been graced with the knowledge of Christ and the love of God bring it the truth it longs to hear.

"Holy Spirit, give us clarity and conviction about the holy name, the works, the life, the death, and the resurrection of Jesus our Savior. Give us clarity about how to speak with other people about these truths in a way that will touch their hearts and open them to the love of God shown through Jesus Christ."

Acts 13:44-52

44 The next sabbath almost the whole city gathered together to hear the word of God. 45 But when the Jews saw the multitudes, they were filled with jealousy, and contradicted what was spoken by Paul, and reviled him. 46 And Paul and Barnabas spoke out boldly, saying, "It was necessary that the word of God should be spoken first to you. Since you thrust it from you, and judge yourselves unworthy of eternal life, behold, we turn to the Gentiles. 47 For so the Lord has commanded us, saying, 'I have set you to be a light for the Gentiles, that you may bring salvation to the uttermost parts of the earth.' "
48 And when the Gentiles heard this, they were glad and glorified the word of God; and as many as were ordained to eternal life believed.
49 And the word of the Lord spread throughout all the region. 50 But the Jews incited the devout women of high standing and the leading men of the city, and stirred up persecution against Paul and Barnabas, and drove them out of their district. 51 But they shook off the dust from their feet against them, and went to Iconium. 52 And the disciples were filled with joy and with the Holy Spirit.

Paul and Barnabas ran into stiff opposition when they continued to proclaim the gospel at Antioch of Pisidia. Despite this persecution (Acts 13:45), they continued to speak the word of the gospel, filled with joy and the Holy Spirit (13:52). How, we wonder, could these two men, faced with such hostility, persevere in their preaching of the gospel of salvation?

The Holy Spirit creates within those who believe in the death and resurrection of Jesus Christ a desire for all people to come to salvation. Jesus gave his disciples the command to preach the gospel to all creation (Matthew 28:18-20; Mark 16:15). The power to preach comes from allowing the Spirit of Jesus to show us the world through his eyes. In our own strength and subject to our own emotions, we will not be able to endure the hostility we are likely to encounter.

How easy it is to feel angry and frustrated when a friend, spouse, or relative rejects the gospel when we speak to them about it. Even though we want them to receive the fullness of the life that Christ gives, our emotions cloud our objectivity. We react with anger and resentment instead of asking Jesus to pour his love into our hearts and theirs.

Jesus sent the Holy Spirit to enable us to proclaim the gospel. It is essential that we keep our eyes fixed on Jesus, he who loved the world so much that he gave his life to save it (John 3:16). Let us examine ourselves to see if we truly have the love of God in our hearts for those we are seeking to evangelize.

"Lord Jesus, you came into the world so that all might receive salvation through your death and resurrection. You sent the Holy Spirit to enable us to preach the gospel to all people. We repent of all the anger, discouragement, and frustration we sometimes feel toward those we try to evangelize. Anoint us with the Holy Spirit so that we may proclaim your truth with joy and confidence."

Acts 14:1-7

¹ Now at Iconium they entered together into the Jewish synagogue, and so spoke that a great company believed, both of Jews and of Greeks. ² But the unbelieving Jews stirred up the Gentiles and poisoned their minds against the brethren. ³ So they remained for a long time, speaking boldly for the Lord, who bore witness to the word of his grace, granting signs and wonders to be done by their hands. ⁴ But the people of the city were divided; some sided with the Jews, and some with the apostles. ⁵ When an attempt was made by both Gentiles and Jews, with their rulers, to molest them and to stone them, ⁶ they learned of it and fled to Lystra and Derbe, cities of Lycaonia, and to the surrounding country; ⁷ and there they preached the gospel.

The disciples were filled with joy and with the Holy Spirit. (Acts 13:52)

After being subjected to violent abuse and expulsion from Pisidia, Antioch, and Iconium, how could Paul and Barnabas be filled with joy and the Holy Spirit? The answer lies in the fact that they had fixed deeply in their hearts a sense of God's divine plan and purposes for his people. They had a heavenly perspective on life.

While persecution is an element of the proclamation of the gospel which many Christians do not understand, these men must have had a sense of Jesus' words to his followers: "If they persecuted me, they will persecute you" (John 15:20); "Blessed are you when men revile you and persecute you and utter all kinds of evil against you falsely on my account. Rejoice and be glad, for your reward is great in heaven, for so men persecuted the prophets who were before you" (Matthew 5:11-12).

The early Christians were able to endure persecution without losing their joy or the presence of the Spirit because they were clear about what

God had already done and what he had promised to do in the future. Paul was equally clear about the promises of God that would be fulfilled for him in heaven: "I press on toward the goal for the prize of the upward call of God in Christ Jesus. Let those of you who are mature be thus minded" (Philippians 3:14-15).

We may not be hounded from place to place like Barnabas and Paul, but the hostility we may experience from neighbors, family members, or fellow workers when we share the truth of the good news of Jesus can be just as real as that which they faced. We must be as focused on heavenly realities as were these men if we are to maintain our joy in the face of trials.

"Gracious Father, despite anything we face, may we be filled with joy and the Holy Spirit. Through that same Spirit, help us to focus on your love and the plan you have for your people through Christ Jesus our Lord."

Acts 14:8-18

[8] Now at Lystra there was a man sitting, who could not use his feet; he was a cripple from birth, who had never walked. [9] He listened to Paul speaking; and Paul, looking intently at him and seeing that he had faith to be made well, [10] said in a loud voice, "Stand upright on your feet." And he sprang up and walked. [11] And when the crowds saw what Paul had done, they lifted up their voices, saying in Lycaonian, "The gods have come down to us in the likeness of men!" [12] Barnabas they called Zeus, and Paul, because he was the chief speaker, they called Hermes. [13] And the priest of Zeus, whose temple was in front of the city, brought oxen and garlands to the gates and wanted to offer sacrifice with the people. [14] But when the apostles Barnabas and Paul heard of it, they tore their garments and rushed out among the multitude, crying, [15] "Men, why are you doing this? We also are men,

of like nature with you, and bring you good news, that you should turn from these vain things to a living God who made the heaven and the earth and the sea and all that is in them. [16] In past generations he allowed all the nations to walk in their own ways; [17] yet he did not leave himself without witness, for he did good and gave you from heaven rains and fruitful seasons, satisfying your hearts with food and gladness." [18] With these words they scarcely restrained the people from offering sacrifice to them. ✎

I magine Paul's shock when the people of Lystra called him Hermes! It all seemed so innocent at first. Paul had sensed that the lame man had the faith to be healed, so he spoke boldly and told the man to stand up. But the onlookers did not understand that they had just seen the power of Jesus working *through* Paul. Instead, they assumed that Greek gods had performed this miracle—and that Paul and Barnabas *were* gods! These two apostles must have wondered where they had gone wrong! Through this humorous situation, Luke showed the foibles of our humanness. The unexpected *can* happen, even when we are doing our best to serve the Lord.

Paul and Barnabas were not the first to perform a miracle and experience the adulation of a crowd. Peter and John excited onlookers when they healed a man before entering the temple (Acts 3:1-14); Jesus had to escape from a crowd that wanted to make him king because he miraculously fed five thousand people (John 6:1-15).

Should fear of the unexpected keep us from trying to preach the gospel? No. These gospel stories remind us that the fruit of our efforts should always be credited to God's power. There is much we can learn from every experience, however unexpected. Paul, though probably mortified by what occurred, learned more deeply how to preach Jesus to pagans—and how *not* to. Good came from the situation, even though not exactly as Paul had planned.

Trial and error—even humor—have a place in following Jesus. We learn much in church, through the Scriptures, and in prayer. But let's not forget that we also learn as we listen to the Holy Spirit and take risks in reaching out to others in Jesus' name. God never condemns us for trying. He only asks that we remain teachable. We can take comfort in Jesus' promise that "the Counselor, the Holy Spirit, whom the Father will send in my name, he will teach you all things, and bring to your remembrance all that I have said to you" (John 14:26).

"Holy Spirit, we know that sometimes things do not turn out as we think they should. Let us approach such situations with open hearts so that opportunities to speak of your greatness can bring your glory to the world."

Acts 14:19-28

[19] But Jews came there from Antioch and Iconium; and having persuaded the people, they stoned Paul and dragged him out of the city, supposing that he was dead. [20] But when the disciples gathered about him, he rose up and entered the city; and on the next day he went on with Barnabas to Derbe. [21] When they had preached the gospel to that city and had made many disciples, they returned to Lystra and to Iconium and to Antioch, [22] strengthening the souls of the disciples, exhorting them to continue in the faith, and saying that through many tribulations we must enter the kingdom of God. [23] And when they had appointed elders for them in every church, with prayer and fasting they committed them to the Lord in whom they believed. [24] Then they passed through Pisidia, and came to Pamphylia. [25] And when they had spoken the word in Perga, they went down to Attalia; [26] and from there they sailed to Antioch, where they had been

commended to the grace of God for the work which they had fulfilled. [27] And when they arrived, they gathered the church together and declared all that God had done with them, and how he had opened a door of faith to the Gentiles. [28] And they remained no little time with the disciples. 🖎

Paul and Barnabas worked carefully and with perseverance to build the church in Asia Minor. They were not just traveling preachers who paid one brief visit and then disappeared. They spent time in each city, making many disciples (Acts 14:21) and, despite hardship, they returned to encourage them and strengthen the churches. They were driven out of Antioch and then forced to flee Iconium. In Lystra the people stoned Paul and dragged him out of the city, leaving him for dead. Then they moved on to Derbe (13:50; 14:5,19-20).

In each place, the apostles were welcomed at first, and many people—Jews and Greeks—came to believe in Christ. But then opponents would arise and turn people against them. Given such persecutions, why did these apostles return the same way they came, visiting again the cities that had treated them so badly?

Paul and Barnabas knew that unless the new converts to Christianity were encouraged and taught, they couldn't hold on to their new faith in the midst of opposition. Consequently, they set about "strengthening the souls of the disciples, exhorting them to continue in the faith, and saying that through many tribulations we must enter the kingdom of God" (Acts 14:22). So great was their desire to help that they returned even to Lystra, where Paul had previously been stoned!

The apostles understood that suffering and persecution were part of their new life. It was the way Jesus himself embraced (Luke 24:26), and it was a specific part of Paul's own calling (Acts 9:16). They returned because they did not want to leave the new disciples without practical help in building their newly founded church. They appointed elders to oversee each community after Paul and Barnabas had gone. This structure reflects the church order that Paul himself was under, having been sent out on this missionary journey by the church at Antioch and reporting back to them upon his return (14:27).

We can learn a lesson from Paul and Barnabas in whatever vocation we are called to. As they willingly accepted God's calling and leading, so too can we. When we do the tasks God asks of us each day, let us do so with the same care and dedication that these first apostles had. And finally, when we face hardship or persecution, let us rejoice in the knowledge that we are walking the same path as Jesus, and that he will never abandon us.

The Council of Jerusalem

ACTS
15:1-35

Acts 15:1-6

[1] But some men came down from Judea and were teaching the brethren, "Unless you are circumcised according to the custom of Moses, you cannot be saved." [2] And when Paul and Barnabas had no small dissension and debate with them, Paul and Barnabas and some of the others were appointed to go up to Jerusalem to the apostles and the elders about this question. [3] So, being sent on their way by the church, they passed through both Phoenicia and Samaria, reporting the conversion of the Gentiles, and they gave great joy to all the brethren. [4] When they came to Jerusalem, they were welcomed by the church and the apostles and the elders, and they declared all that God had done with them. [5] But some believers who belonged to the party of the Pharisees rose up, and said, "It is necessary to circumcise them, and to charge them to keep the law of Moses."
[6] The apostles and the elders were gathered together to consider this matter.

Paul and Barnabas returned to Antioch after a missionary journey in which they logged over a thousand miles as they preached the gospel throughout Asia Minor. In at least four cities (Antioch of Pisidia, Iconium, Lystra, and Derbe), their message was received with open hearts, and they established new churches, composed of both Jews and Gentiles. Throughout their journey, the Spirit was at work through them, changing people's hearts, healing the sick, and delivering the oppressed.

Now, having returned to Antioch and reporting the success of the mission, Paul and Barnabas faced a new challenge which threatened the whole church: what to do with the Gentiles who were becoming Christians. Should they be forced to accept circumcision and become

Jews first? Should they be admitted into the church at all? From ancient times, it was understood that God's favor was reserved for his chosen people (Psalm 147:19-20). At the same time, however, as prophecy developed, the Lord made it clear that he wanted all nations to come to know his love (Amos 9:11-12; Isaiah 49:6). How should they bring these two strands together?

The question of the inclusion of Gentiles was no small issue. "Dissension and debate" arose (Acts 15:2), and the elders at Antioch— a church composed of Jews and Greeks—sent Paul, Barnabas, and some other representatives to Jerusalem where they could discuss the matter with the elders of the church.

In every age, the church faces challenges that can either undermine its calling or cause it to shine more brightly in a darkened world. Today, in places like China, Rwanda, and Cuba, the church faces persecution; in Haiti and the Balkans, crumbling societies; and in the more comfortable Western countries, the cheapening of human life that comes from an emphasis on material gain. In all these situations, the church's elders are drawn together to seek the wisdom of the Spirit. Councils, synods, conferences, and retreats continue today, just as they did in Jerusalem and Antioch ages ago. In these gatherings, the leaders of the church continue to seek the guidance of the Spirit in their labors so that the cause of Christ might advance on earth.

"Father, we thank you that you have never abandoned the church and that even today you are working in our midst. We pray for the church today, that it may respond to the challenges of the Holy Spirit in full fidelity to the eternal gospel of Jesus Christ."

Acts 15:7-21

[7] And after there had been much debate, Peter rose and said to them, "Brethren, you know that in the early days God made choice among you, that by my mouth the Gentiles should hear the word of the gospel and believe. [8] And God who knows the heart bore witness to them, giving them the Holy Spirit just as he did to us; [9] and he made no distinction between us and them, but cleansed their hearts by faith. [10] Now therefore why do you make trial of God by putting a yoke upon the neck of the disciples which neither our fathers nor we have been able to bear? [11] But we believe that we shall be saved through the grace of the Lord Jesus, just as they will."

[12] And all the assembly kept silence; and they listened to Barnabas and Paul as they related what signs and wonders God had done through them among the Gentiles. [13] After they finished speaking, James replied, "Brethren, listen to me. [14] Simeon has related how God first visited the Gentiles, to take out of them a people for his name. [15] And with this the words of the prophets agree, as it is written, [16] 'After this I will return, and I will rebuild the dwelling of David, which has fallen; I will rebuild its ruins, and I will set it up, [17] that the rest of men may seek the Lord, and all the Gentiles who are called by my name, [18] says the Lord, who has made these things known from of old.' [19] Therefore my judgment is that we should not trouble those of the Gentiles who turn to God, [20] but should write to them to abstain from the pollutions of idols and from unchastity and from what is strangled and from blood. [21] For from early generations Moses has had in every city those who preach him, for he is read every sabbath in the synagogues."

The Council of Jerusalem was a decisive turning point for the early church. Because of controversy stirred up by zealous Jewish Christians, the elders convened to discern the place of gentile Christians in the community of believers. Would they be officially admitted, and under what conditions? Given the Jews' heritage—the Scriptures, the prophets, the patriarchs, the temple—it may not be hard to understand why some objected to the Gentiles' inclusion. But a careful reading of the Hebrew Scriptures, especially the writings after the Babylonian exile, gives a bigger perspective on God's intentions.

In the eighth century B.C., Isaiah prophesied that Mount Zion would become the gathering place for all people, where all nations would be brought into his kingdom (Isaiah 2:2-4). Two hundred years later, through a disciple of Isaiah, the Lord promised: "I am coming to gather all nations and tongues; and they shall come and see my glory" (Isaiah 66:18). And Zechariah prophesied: "In those days ten men from the nations of every tongue shall take hold of the robe of a Jew, saying, 'Let us go with you, for we have heard that God is with you'" (Zechariah 8:23).

With the outpouring of the Spirit at Pentecost, these wondrous promises of God began to find their fulfillment. Jesus' resurrection has broken down the dividing wall between Gentile and Jew (Ephesians 2:11-15). Everyone can become beloved sons and daughters, with the promise of eternal life in the future and the gift of the Holy Spirit right now. The Jewish law, God's tool of preparation for the Messiah, has been superseded by the "law of the Spirit of life in Christ Jesus" (Romans 8:2-3).

From the time of Peter's vision on a rooftop in Joppa and his encounter with Cornelius (Acts 10), God had been preparing the apostles for the unthinkable. Because of their openness to the Spirit and their humble obedience to God, they were able to perceive the "new thing" (Isaiah 43:19) that God was doing, and so open the doors of the church to everyone to believe and be baptized.

"Father, we rejoice today that you are always faithful to your promises. Help us to look upon all people with love, just as you do."

Acts 15:22-35

[22] Then it seemed good to the apostles and the elders, with the whole church, to choose men from among them and send them to Antioch with Paul and Barnabas. They sent Judas called Barsabbas, and Silas, leading men among the brethren, [23] with the following letter: "The brethren, both the apostles and the elders, to the brethren who are of the Gentiles in Antioch and Syria and Cilicia, greeting. [24] Since we have heard that some persons from us have troubled you with words, unsettling your minds, although we gave them no instructions, [25] it has seemed good to us, having come to one accord, to choose men and send them to you with our beloved Barnabas and Paul, [26] men who have risked their lives for the sake of our Lord Jesus Christ. [27] We have therefore sent Judas and Silas, who themselves will tell you the same things by word of mouth. [28] For it has seemed good to the Holy Spirit and to us to lay upon you no greater burden than these necessary things: [29] that you abstain from what has been sacrificed to idols and from blood and from what is strangled and from unchastity. If you keep yourselves from these, you will do well. Farewell."

[30] So when they were sent off, they went down to Antioch; and having gathered the congregation together, they delivered the letter. [31] And when they read it, they rejoiced at the exhortation. [32] And Judas and Silas, who were themselves prophets, exhorted the brethren with many words and strengthened them. [33] And after they had spent some time, they were sent off in peace by the brethren to those who had sent them. [35] But Paul and Barnabas remained in Antioch, teaching and preaching the word of the Lord, with many others also.

God speaks to us through his Holy Spirit. Because he does, we—as members of Christ's body—are able to carry out his will on earth. These momentous truths have been attested to throughout salvation history, right up to the present time. This is the heritage of every Christian who has ever been touched by God.

At the Council of Jerusalem, the Holy Spirit led the fledgling church in one of its first major decisions. Put yourself in the shoes of the men assembled there. Peter, Paul, James, and others had committed their whole lives in return for the Lord's love for them. They knew one another as brothers in Christ and wanted to trust, yet they differed over how Gentiles should relate to the Jewish law. Everyone meant well, but how could they discern God's will in this situation?

"It has seemed good to the Holy Spirit and to us to lay upon you no greater burden than these necessary things" (Acts 15:28). The apostles knew that the Holy Spirit would make God's will known. Their differences were resolved not because one side was more persuasive than the other, but because the Spirit of God revealed to them what was pleasing to Christ. Thus the plan of God in heaven was accomplished in his church on earth.

The unity which the council delegates experienced was also a work of the Holy Spirit. They didn't just use their minds to come to common agreement; they relied on the gifts of knowledge, wisdom, and discernment that are spiritual in origin (1 Corinthians 12:4-10). Similarly, our unity as Christians is not based on common likes, attitudes, or rituals. The deep unity we experience as the body of Christ comes because the Spirit has been poured into each of our hearts, instilling in our varied personalities a true love for Jesus.

"Father in heaven, thank you for teaching us through your Holy Spirit to love your Son. Thank you for speaking to us regarding matters, both great and small, in our lives and in the life of the church. Give us the grace always to listen to your voice in order that Jesus may be glorified in heaven and on earth."

Breaking New Ground

ACTS
15:36–17:34

Acts 15:36-41

36 And after some days Paul said to Barnabas, "Come, let us return and visit the brethren in every city where we proclaimed the word of the Lord, and see how they are." 37 And Barnabas wanted to take with them John called Mark. 38 But Paul thought best not to take with them one who had withdrawn from them in Pamphylia, and had not gone with them to the work. 39 And there arose a sharp contention, so that they separated from each other; Barnabas took Mark with him and sailed away to Cyprus, 40 but Paul chose Silas and departed, being commended by the brethren to the grace of the Lord. 41 And he went through Syria and Cilicia, strengthening the churches.

Our God is absolutely amazing! He loves us. He lives in us. He uses us to bring others to him. In those who keep their hearts humble, no weakness or fallibility stymies him. And we mustn't allow any to hinder us, either. Sin is no obstacle to God. After all, he was able to use Paul and Barnabas and John Mark. Even those pillars of the early church were weak and occasionally contentious, like the rest of us. It's easy to idealize the apostles and saints and place them on a pedestal. But just like us, they too were subject to temptation. And, just like us, they too gave in to temptation upon occasion.

Barnabas and Paul were prominent, highly respected church leaders. Paul may be better known as the one to bring the gospel to the Gentiles, but it was Barnabas who introduced Paul to the apostles, recruited him to minister in Antioch, went on missionary tours with him, and stood up for him before the Jerusalem council. Together, these two men had a vast impact on the church, and even on the ancient world itself. Still, they had their faults and erred just as we do. And they kept going. They continued to love and serve the Lord.

Your mistakes and sins matter less than your response to them. Do you believe this? Remember, God has given you the precious gifts of repentance, forgiveness, and reconciliation. What a joy it is to be able to repent! When you do so, sin doesn't have the final word—the blood of Jesus does (1 John 1:7). Through repentance and faith in his blood, we can be reconciled to God and to one another. Even estrangements like the one between Paul and Barnabas don't have to persist. All we need is the humility to say, "I'm sorry," or "I forgive you."

Brothers and sisters, let's be honest about ourselves. We are all prone to sin and mistakes. We also have a loving Father in heaven who is merciful and gracious (Exodus 34:6). We have the Holy Spirit who heals us and helps recover whatever is lost through sin. Never let sin remain an obstacle between you and God! Never give up serving and loving him! Only be humble, for then God can work in your heart.

"Lord, I praise you for covering me with your blood. Thank you for softening my heart so that I can repent, forgive, and continue following you. I believe that you live in me and will heal and guide me, today and always."

Acts 16:1-10

[1] And he came also to Derbe and to Lystra. A disciple was there, named Timothy, the son of a Jewish woman who was a believer; but his father was a Greek. [2] He was well spoken of by the brethren at Lystra and Iconium. [3] Paul wanted Timothy to accompany him; and he took him and circumcised him because of the Jews that were in those places, for they all knew that his father was a Greek. [4] As they went on their way through the cities, they delivered to them for observance the decisions which had been reached by the apostles and elders who were at Jerusalem. [5] So the churches were strengthened in the faith,

and they increased in numbers daily.

[6] And they went through the region of Phrygia and Galatia, having been forbidden by the Holy Spirit to speak the word in Asia. [7] And when they had come opposite Mysia, they attempted to go into Bithynia, but the Spirit of Jesus did not allow them; [8] so, passing by Mysia, they went down to Troas. [9] And a vision appeared to Paul in the night: a man of Macedonia was standing beseeching him and saying, "Come over to Macedonia and help us." [10] And when he had seen the vision, immediately we sought to go on into Macedonia, concluding that God had called us to preach the gospel to them.

I t all looks so simple when we read Acts of the Apostles. The fledgling church begins in Jerusalem among the Jews. Then it spreads to surrounding areas—first to Jews, then to the "God-fearers" who were Gentiles who embraced the God of Abraham but not all the stipulations of the Jewish law, and finally to the Gentiles. From there Paul and various companions carry the faith to Cyprus and parts of Asia Minor. Now by a work of the Spirit, their plans change and they enter Europe.

But it wasn't quite so clear or simple then. Paul had planned to embark on bold evangelistic travels north and east toward Asia, but he and Silas encountered roadblocks which Paul discerned to be from the Holy Spirit. After several aborted forays into Asia, the Spirit revealed to Paul that he was to direct his evangelism westward, toward Greece and Europe (Acts 16:6-10). It was on this journey that Paul founded some of the communities prominent in the New Testament: Philippi, Thessalonica, and Corinth. This little history teaches us about living according to the Spirit's guidance.

First, we need to make plans. In our work as Christians, we need to determine what is right and reasonable to do in light of all that God has taught us and shown us. We have to establish goals and set a course. Our initial plans may be redirected by God, just as Paul's were. That doesn't mean that planning is not a good thing to do; it just means that sometimes plans have to be revised. The Lord wants us to take the initiative in the work we do for him, but our planning should be done in collaboration with the Holy Spirit, and we must remain open to divine intervention.

Second, the Spirit may refine and improve upon our plans, so we need to be listening for his voice and direction. Paul's first plans to visit Asia were not made apart from God, but his efforts bore unimaginable fruit as he listened to the Spirit and obeyed. The spread of Christianity through Europe in the succeeding centuries was due in part to Paul's Spirit-led decisions.

"Holy Spirit, teach us to plan as best we can, and to alter those plans as you might direct. Lead us into God's presence more regularly, so that we can listen for his voice. We know we will receive unexpected blessings when we follow you."

Acts 16:11-15

[11] Setting sail therefore from Troas, we made a direct voyage to Samothrace, and the following day to Ne-apolis, [12] and from there to Philippi, which is the leading city of the district of Macedonia, and a Roman colony. We remained in this city some days; [13] and on the sabbath day we went outside the gate to the riverside, where we supposed there was a place of prayer; and we sat down and spoke to the women who had come together. [14] One who heard us was a woman named Lydia, from the city of Thyatira, a seller of purple goods, who was a worshiper of God. The Lord opened her heart to give heed to

what was said by Paul. [15] And when she was baptized, with her household, she besought us, saying, "If you have judged me to be faithful to the Lord, come to my house and stay." And she prevailed upon us. ✦

On the bank of a river, a group of women gathered to pray and observe the sabbath together. Most likely some were Jews, while others were God-fearing Gentiles attracted to Judaism's morality and belief in the one God. Among the latter was Lydia, a merchant who sold costly purple-dyed fabrics, perhaps even traveling from city to city in the region that we know today as Turkey.

Lydia was a successful businesswoman and persistent in her pursuit of God. She hungered for knowledge of the truth and sought it first in the Jewish way of life. Her thirst for truth was strong enough that she remained attached to Judaism even in Philippi, a Roman colony where the Jewish faith appears to have languished amid the competition from other religions.

On this particular sabbath, Lydia and her fellow worshippers were joined by Paul and his companions who had gone outside the walls of Philippi looking for a place of prayer. When Paul sat down and spoke to the women, the Lord opened Lydia's heart to heed his words about the life and love of God which was available to them in Jesus (Acts 16:14).

We don't know how the others reacted, but Lydia responded to God's grace wholeheartedly. In a spirit of openness to the truth, she embraced Jesus as the Messiah, committing her life to faith in him whom Paul proclaimed. She sought and received baptism for herself and her household (Acts 16:15). Lydia then generously entreated Paul and his fellow travelers to stay with her while they remained in Philippi.

God moved in Lydia, stirring up a longing for the truth. As Paul spoke, God opened her heart to see and welcome Jesus, to accept the truth and commit herself to Christ through baptism. The Lord kindled gratitude in her heart, and she responded by sharing generously with Paul and the other evangelists. When she yielded to God, he worked in her to help build the church in Europe. God wants to work in us too; he wants to touch us just as he did Lydia.

"Lord, you blessed Lydia with a spirit of openness, hunger for the truth, and a generous heart. In return she responded to your grace. Inspire us with that same openness and desire so that we may always seek you, receive you, and serve others out of gratitude for your life in us."

Acts 16:16-21

[16] As we were going to the place of prayer, we were met by a slave girl who had a spirit of divination and brought her owners much gain by soothsaying. [17] She followed Paul and us, crying, "These men are servants of the Most High God, who proclaim to you the way of salvation." [18] And this she did for many days. But Paul was annoyed, and turned and said to the spirit, "I charge you in the name of Jesus Christ to come out of her." And it came out that very hour.
[19] But when her owners saw that their hope of gain was gone, they seized Paul and Silas and dragged them into the market place before the rulers; [20] and when they had brought them to the magistrates they said, "These men are Jews and they are disturbing our city. [21] They advocate customs which it is not lawful for us Romans to accept or practice."

Doesn't it strike you as a bit odd that the demon who had possessed this young woman openly confessed that Paul and Silas were "servants of the Most High God, who proclaim to you the way of salvation" (Acts 16:17)? It might help to know that there are a number of occasions in the New Testament where evil spirits acknowledge the truth and action of God. At the very beginning of Jesus' ministry, for instance, a man possessed by an evil spirit declares him to be "the Holy One of God" until Jesus silences the demon (Luke 4:33-35).

There are many voices in this world offering "wisdom," but not all of them speak the truth and wisdom that leads to eternal life. Some people are drawn to divination because they want to know what the future holds for them, but the only secure future is the one Jesus promises those who follow him. That's why Paul wanted to see this girl freed from the spirit of divination. Paul also wanted to avoid any confusion among Christians as to the true source of guidance and direction for their lives. We all need spiritual discernment so that we can distinguish the voice of Christ from the voices of the world.

The evil one uses any means he can to rob us of our trust in God and his word. When worries and troubles beset you, do you yield to thoughts of irrational fear and anxiety, or do you turn to God with trust in his love and care for you? When someone injures you, do you give in to voices of hatred and retaliation? Or do you try your best to forgive the person and hold no resentments?

God wants the fruit of his Spirit to operate in our lives (Galatians 5:22-23). He wants his love, peace, and joy to influence the way we think and act. If you find a "spirit" of anger, lust, or fear trying to take control of your life, turn to Jesus and ask for his help. He will give you the strength to resist evil with good. Jesus is always ready to set you free from all that would keep you from his love. Ask the Lord to fill you with his Spirit that you may grow in the fruit which he desires for you.

"Lord, fill me with your Holy Spirit and direct my thoughts and actions, that I may discern what is true and choose what is good."

Acts 16:22-40

22 The crowd joined in attacking them; and the magistrates tore the garments off them and gave orders to beat them with rods. 23 And when they had inflicted many blows upon them, they threw them into prison, charging the jailer to keep them safely. 24 Having received this charge, he put them into the inner prison and fastened their feet in the stocks.

25 But about midnight Paul and Silas were praying and singing hymns to God, and the prisoners were listening to them, 26 and suddenly there was a great earthquake, so that the foundations of the prison were shaken; and immediately all the doors were opened and every one's fetters were unfastened. 27 When the jailer woke and saw that the prison doors were open, he drew his sword and was about to kill himself, supposing that the prisoners had escaped. 28 But Paul cried with a loud voice, "Do not harm yourself, for we are all here." 29 And he called for lights and rushed in, and trembling with fear he fell down before Paul and Silas, 30 and brought them out and said, "Men, what must I do to be saved?" 31 And they said, "Believe in the Lord Jesus, and you will be saved, you and your household." 32 And they spoke the word of the Lord to him and to all that were in his house. 33 And he took them the same hour of the night, and washed their wounds, and he was baptized at once, with all his family. 34 Then he brought them up into his house, and set food before them; and he rejoiced with all his household that he had believed in God.

35 But when it was day, the magistrates sent the police, saying, "Let those men go." 36 And the jailer reported the words to Paul, saying, "The magistrates have sent to let you go; now therefore come out and go in peace." 37 But Paul said to them, "They have beaten us publicly, uncondemned, men who are Roman citizens, and have thrown us into prison; and do they now cast us out secretly? No! let them come themselves and take us out." 38 The police reported these words to the

magistrates, and they were afraid when they heard that they were Roman citizens; [39] so they came and apologized to them. And they took them out and asked them to leave the city. [40] So they went out of the prison, and visited Lydia; and when they had seen the brethren, they exhorted them and departed. ✍

T est yourself: How were Paul and Silas ultimately released from prison in Philippi? Your first answer would probably be that there was an earthquake, the chains fell from their feet, they prevented the guard from committing suicide, went home with him . . . and then were free. Actually, Paul and Silas went back to the prison and were freed only the next day by order of a magistrate (Acts 16:35-36). In other words, having been miraculously freed from an unjust imprisonment, Paul and Silas voluntarily resubmitted themselves to that very same imprisonment! This tells us a lot about the kind of men these two evangelists were.

First, they were men who were led by the Spirit. Rather than presuming that the earthquake had occurred solely to free them from their chains, they recognized that the Spirit was giving them a chance to proclaim the good news. The fact that the earthquake did not result in their freedom shows that part of God's plan was to save the jailer and his family! Who knows what role this family was to play in the growth of the newborn church in Philippi after Paul and Silas left?

Second, it shows that Paul and Silas were men who put the preaching of the gospel ahead of everything. The fact that the jailer pleaded with them, saying, "Men, what must I do to be saved?" (Acts 16:30), indicates that he had probably already heard at least part of the gospel from their lips. The perseverance of these two men of God in proclaiming the gospel of Jesus Christ resulted in this man's knowing where he could turn to hear the words of life.

Finally, it is clear that Silas and Paul were not acting alone. God's purpose was to see the gospel preached and to save the jailer and his family through it. The confident prayer and worship of Paul and Silas in the prison was accompanied by God's very real presence and his intervention in their lives.

In all this we can see the principles of Christian living upon which we can rely. Obedience to the Spirit, perseverance in proclaiming the gospel under all circumstances, and confidence that God is working with us in our efforts to evangelize—these are our assets as sons and daughters of God. Let us put them to use as we share the truth of Jesus Christ.

Acts 17:1-15

[1] Now when they had passed through Amphipolis and Apollonia, they came to Thessalonica, where there was a synagogue of the Jews. [2] And Paul went in, as was his custom, and for three weeks he argued with them from the scriptures, [3] explaining and proving that it was necessary for the Christ to suffer and to rise from the dead, and saying, "This Jesus, whom I proclaim to you, is the Christ." [4] And some of them were persuaded, and joined Paul and Silas; as did a great many of the devout Greeks and not a few of the leading women. [5] But the Jews were jealous, and taking some wicked fellows of the rabble, they gathered a crowd, set the city in an uproar, and attacked the house of Jason, seeking to bring them out to the people. [6] And when they could not find them, they dragged Jason and some of the brethren before the city authorities, crying, "These men who have turned the world upside down have come here also, [7] and Jason has received them; and they are all acting against the decrees of Caesar, saying that there is another king, Jesus." [8] And the people and the city authorities were disturbed when they heard this. [9] And when they had taken security from Jason and the rest, they let them go.

[10] The brethren immediately sent Paul and Silas away by night to Beroea; and when they arrived they went into the Jewish synagogue. [11] Now these Jews were more noble than those in Thessalonica, for they received the word with all eagerness, examining the scriptures daily to see if these things were so. [12] Many of them therefore believed, with not a few Greek women of high standing as well as men. [13] But when the Jews of Thessalonica learned that the word of God was proclaimed by Paul at Beroea also, they came there too, stirring up and inciting the crowds. [14] Then the brethren immediately sent Paul off on his way to the sea, but Silas and Timothy remained there. [15] Those who conducted Paul brought him as far as Athens; and receiving a command for Silas and Timothy to come to him as soon as possible, they departed. ✺

As this passage demonstrates, whenever he entered a new city, Paul began by preaching in the synagogues, telling his fellow Jews that Jesus is the fulfillment of the Law and the prophets. And, as we see in numerous passages in Acts, some of his listeners were won over and others resisted and caused trouble. But the church was established nonetheless, and the people continued to hold fast to the faith proclaimed to them.

If Paul's message was unchanging, why were there so many different responses among those who listened to him? Some "received the word with all eagerness, examining the Scriptures daily to see if these things were so" (Acts 17:11), while others "became jealous and formed a mob" (17:5). How could some come to faith in Christ while others became cynical or even hostile?

Paul may have proclaimed the gospel boldly, but it wasn't the force of his argument that brought people to faith. First and foremost, it was the *work of the Holy Spirit*. He is always the governing principle in any true effort of evangelization. With the Spirit working in them, the people read Scripture and sought God's wisdom, keeping their hearts open to any new revelation that the Spirit wanted to give them. Beyond the arguments, testimonies, and appeals to reason, the Spirit revealed the truth to those who eagerly sought it.

With the Holy Spirit dwelling in them, the new Christians had what they needed to survive and grow. The Thessalonian Christians who accepted Paul's message faced massive opposition from the Jews in the city. In addition, they quickly lost their leaders, Paul and Silas (Acts 17:5,10). Yet, we know from Paul's letters that the church there thrived (1 Thessalonians 1:1-10). That's because Paul and Silas had done the most important thing: They introduced the Thessalonians to Jesus and opened the door for them to receive the Holy Spirit.

By remaining open to the Holy Spirit and not relying only on the words of other people, we too can grow and mature in our faith. Are you eager to seek the truth in Scripture? Do you hunger for God's wisdom? Do you allow the Holy Spirit to soften your heart and give you new revelations? Do you pray for the Holy Spirit to increase in your life? In all these ways, we too, like the Thessalonians, can become spiritually healthy, thriving Christians who bring life and love to their communities of faith.

"Lord Jesus, I commit my life to you this day. I give you my all as I receive all of you. May I see you for who you really are, and may I proclaim you to a world that doesn't know you."

Acts 17:16-21

[16] Now while Paul was waiting for them at Athens, his spirit was provoked within him as he saw that the city was full of idols. [17] So he argued in the synagogue with the Jews and the devout persons, and in the market place every day with those who chanced to be there. [18] Some also of the Epicurean and Stoic philosophers met him. And some said, "What would this babbler say?" Others said, "He seems to be a preacher of foreign divinities"—because he preached Jesus and the resurrection. [19] And they took hold of him and brought him to the Are-opagus, saying, "May we know what this new teaching is which you present? [20] For you bring some strange things to our ears; we wish to know therefore what these things mean." [20] Now all the Athenians and the foreigners who lived there spent their time in nothing except telling or hearing something new. ✺

Ever the innovator, Paul took on a new direction in Athens. Rather than just speaking in the local synagogue or some other religious gathering, as was his custom, he went to the marketplace, the hub of Athens' business and social life. To get a sense of what this was like, try to imagine yourself approaching people in your local mall and offering to tell them about Jesus. That's quite a difference from offering a Bible study in your parish or helping out with the youth group!

At places like the synagogue, people have two things in common: They believe in God and are there to pursue him. But in the marketplace, anything could happen, and this was especially the case in Athens. Where else could a person in the first century find Stoic and Epicurean philosophers to dispute with? Paul was in an alien environment and couldn't draw on his stronger traits, such as his familiarity with Hebrew Scriptures. Still, Paul was willing enough and bold enough to engage the Athenians on their terms so that he could win some of them to Christ.

Like Paul, we too must strive to be all things to all people. Sharing our experiences of God's love while shopping, speaking with people in our neighborhood, or even while conducting business at work just might bring someone to Christ who would not otherwise hear the gospel. We don't have to have all the answers, just as Paul wasn't an expert in Greek philosophy. Some may call us "babblers" (Acts 17:18) or not understand our testimony, but our consolation is that God is with us and we truly have good news to share with anyone who will listen.

Let's always remember that Jesus preached all over Galilee and took every opportunity he could find. From a "chance meeting" with a Samaritan woman at a town's well (John 4:1-26) to an impromptu dinner with the "sinners" who were Matthew's friends (Matthew 9:9-13), even to crowds who surrounded him in open fields (Luke 6:17-19), Jesus kept reaching out to those who had eyes to see and ears to hear. We have the same calling and the same Holy Spirit to teach us what to say and how to say it.

"Holy Spirit, I ask for the grace to witness to those who cross my path and who seem unreachable. Give me the boldness to speak of your greatness in new places and in new ways."

Acts 17:22-34

²² So Paul, standing in the middle of the Are-opagus, said: "Men of Athens, I perceive that in every way you are very religious. ²³ For as I passed along, and observed the objects of your worship, I found also an altar with this inscription, 'To an unknown god.' What therefore you worship as unknown, this I proclaim to you. ²⁴ The God who made the world and everything in it, being Lord of heaven and earth, does not live in shrines made by man, ²⁵ nor is he served by human hands, as though he needed anything, since he himself gives to all men life and breath and everything. ²⁶ And he made from one every nation of men to live on all the face of the earth, having determined allotted periods and the boundaries of their habitation, ²⁷ that they should seek God, in the hope that they might feel after him and find him. Yet he is not far from each one of us, ²⁸ for 'In him we live and move and have our being'; as even some of your poets have said, 'For we are indeed his offspring.'

²⁹ "Being then God's offspring, we ought not to think that the Deity is like gold, or silver, or stone, a representation by the art and imagination of man. ³⁰ The times of ignorance God overlooked, but now he commands all men everywhere to repent, ³¹ because he has fixed a day on which he will judge the world in righteousness by a man whom he has appointed, and of this he has given assurance to all men by raising him from the dead."

³² Now when they heard of the resurrection of the dead, some mocked; but others said, "We will hear you again about this." ³³ So Paul went out from among them. ³⁴ But some men joined him and believed, among them Dionysius the Are-opagite and a woman named Damaris and others with them.

From Athen's earliest days, the Areopagus, an amphitheater near the Acropolis, played a central role in the city's government. Before the dawn of democracy, the king's advisory council met there, debating current issues and offering advice to the king. By Paul's time, the Areopagus had diminished in its influence, but it did retain its status as a place of free debate and philosophical inquiry. It was here that Paul was invited to speak, to bring the gospel to the philosophers of Greece. As Luke tells us, this was no easy task. Many came to listen, but only a few came to faith.

Paul's speech before the Areopagus is an example of an effort to move people from a position where they are comfortable to a point where they can place their faith in the gospel. In the Athenians' case, Paul had to move them from a reliance based solely on what their intellect could deduce to a reliance in faith on the promises of God. This was where the philosophers fell short. They would not allow their hearts to be moved and, as a consequence, they remained closed to the working of the Spirit.

St. Columban (c. 540-615), a sixth-century Irish abbot, wrote about the relationship between philosophy and faith:

> Seek the highest knowledge, therefore, not in wordy argument but in integrity of life; not through words but through faith that arises from simplicity of heart and not from the blasphemous conjectures of learned fools. If you seek the ineffable One in human books, he will recede from you further than before; if you seek him through faith, he will abide where he is—at the gates of wisdom, where he abides and may be partially seen. For we believe that God is invisible, though he may be partially seen by the pure of heart. (*Instructions on the Faith*, 1)

At the core of our gospel stands the promise of a new heart and a new spirit, the promise of God's life poured into our hearts (Ezekiel 36:26;

Romans 5:5). Philosophy can be a useful tool in helping people see their need for Christ, but there must be an interior movement away from sin, a movement of the heart toward Christ himself.

Let us seek the Lord today in humility and purity of heart, using our minds as God's precious gift, but looking more broadly, beyond the boundaries of human intellect. Let us open our hearts to Christ and allow him to reign within us.

Corinth and Ephesus

ACTS
18–19

Acts 18:1-11

[1] After this he left Athens and went to Corinth. [2] And he found a Jew named Aquila, a native of Pontus, lately come from Italy with his wife Priscilla, because Claudius had commanded all the Jews to leave Rome. And he went to see them; [3] and because he was of the same trade he stayed with them, and they worked, for by trade they were tentmakers. [4] And he argued in the synagogue every sabbath, and persuaded Jews and Greeks.

[5] When Silas and Timothy arrived from Macedonia, Paul was occupied with preaching, testifying to the Jews that the Christ was Jesus. [6] And when they opposed and reviled him, he shook out his garments and said to them, "Your blood be upon your heads! I am innocent. From now on I will go to the Gentiles." [7] And he left there and went to the house of a man named Titius Justus, a worshiper of God; his house was next door to the synagogue. [8] Crispus, the ruler of the synagogue, believed in the Lord, together with all his household; and many of the Corinthians hearing Paul believed and were baptized. [9] And the Lord said to Paul one night in a vision, "Do not be afraid, but speak and do not be silent; [10] for I am with you, and no man shall attack you to harm you; for I have many people in this city." [11] And he stayed a year and six months, teaching the word of God among them.

Corinth was a cosmopolitan port city on the narrow neck of land that connected mainland Greece and Peleponnesus. Ships could travel from the Aegean Sea to the Adriatic Sea without venturing into the Mediterranean by being wheeled through Corinth across a rock track. This activity generated a valuable source of income for the Corinthians, as well as an opportunity for sailors to indulge themselves in the immoral diversions of the city.

A Roman invasion destroyed the city in 146 B.C. but Julius Caesar reestablished it as a Roman colony one hundred years later. Over that century, Greeks began to resettle in Corinth, so that it became a potpourri of Greek and Latin religion, culture, and philosophy. This was the Corinth to which Paul came in 50 A.D. to preach about Christ.

The specifics of Paul's stay are not known; we only know that he lived there for a year and a half preaching God's word to the people (Acts 18:11). Judging from what we know about Corinth, and what we can derive from Paul's letters to the Corinthians, we must assume that Paul faced a formidable challenge. There were temples in Corinth for almost all of the Greek gods and goddesses. The market area was filled with philosophers espousing the latest wisdom, merchants selling their wares, and shadowy figures profiting from the rampant commerce in immorality.

How did Paul contend with all this? He simply preached the truth of Christ, trusting that this alone could change people's hearts. "When I came among you, brethren, I did not come proclaiming the testimony of God in lofty words or wisdom. For I decided to know nothing among you except Jesus Christ and him crucified . . . that your faith might not rest in the wisdom of men but in the power of God" (1 Corinthians 2:1-2,5). Paul gave the Corinthians an answer to their search for true life that no philosophy or sensual pleasure could ever supply.

Over the course of this time in Corinth, Paul established the beginnings of a church, with committed members turning away from lives of sin and experiencing the Spirit's empowerment to pray, study the Scriptures, and grow in fellowship with one another. He left us a rule of thumb for reaching those we love who seem to be far from God: Preach Christ crucified.

Acts 18:12-21

[12] But when Gallio was proconsul of Achaia, the Jews made a united attack upon Paul and brought him before the tribunal, [13] saying, "This man is persuading men to worship God contrary to the law." [14] But when Paul was about to open his mouth, Gallio said to the Jews, "If it were a matter of wrongdoing or vicious crime, I should have reason to bear with you, O Jews; [15] but since it is a matter of questions about words and names and your own law, see to it yourselves; I refuse to be a judge of these things." [16] And he drove them from the tribunal. [17] And they all seized Sosthenes, the ruler of the synagogue, and beat him in front of the tribunal. But Gallio paid no attention to this. [18] After this Paul stayed many days longer, and then took leave of the brethren and sailed for Syria, and with him Priscilla and Aquila. At Cenchre-ae he cut his hair, for he had a vow. [19] And they came to Ephesus, and he left them there; but he himself went into the synagogue and argued with the Jews. [20] When they asked him to stay for a longer period, he declined; [21] but on taking leave of them he said, "I will return to you if God wills," and he set sail from Ephesus.

W hat an interesting combination of stories! First, Luke gives us a glimpse of one of the many difficulties Paul encountered while preaching the gospel. In this instance, he was accused by some members of the local synagogue before the Roman consul, Gallio, of worshipping in a way contrary to Jewish law. Soon after this, however, Luke tells of Paul cutting his hair in connection with a vow he had made. Most probably, he had taken a special Nazirite vow for a period of time—a sign of being "set apart" for the Lord. For the duration of such a vow, he was bound to refrain from cutting his hair and drinking wine and alcohol (Numbers 6:1-21).

While the specific details and purpose of the vow are unclear, it shows that Paul remained deeply committed to the ways of Judaism despite all the persecution and misunderstandings that many of the Jews had heaped upon him. Luke put these two incidents together to show that *Paul never considered God to have rejected the Jews.* After all, why would he risk so much—including rejection, scorn, and even physical abuse— just to reach the Jewish people if they had been abandoned by God and had no hope of being saved?

Paul loved the covenant God made with Abraham, and his heart's desire was to see the Jewish people embrace the fulfillment of all the promises God had made through Abraham, Moses, and David. He gladly spent himself to bring to them the message of salvation through faith in Christ. With great longing and compassion for his fellow Jews, Paul wrote: "My heart's desire and prayer to God for them is that they may be saved" (Romans 10:1).

Let's examine our own hearts to see if we consider the Jewish people—or anyone else—to be beyond the reach of the Lord. Do we think there are people who have so offended God that our Father just washes his hands of them? Unthinkable! And, as God thinks, so must we. Let's ask Jesus to give us a deeper love for all people. The less judgment there is in the world, the more room the Spirit has to work his wonders.

"God of Abraham, all your promises are fulfilled in Jesus Christ! May the good news of salvation through your Son come to Abraham's descendants and to all peoples everywhere. Widen my heart to embrace all your beloved sons and daughters."

Acts 18:22-28

²² When he had landed at Caesarea, he went up and greeted the church, and then went down to Antioch. ²³ After spending some time there he departed and went from place to place through the region of Galatia and Phrygia, strengthening all the disciples.

²⁴ Now a Jew named Apollos, a native of Alexandria, came to Ephesus. He was an eloquent man, well versed in the scriptures. ²⁵ He had been instructed in the way of the Lord; and being fervent in spirit, he spoke and taught accurately the things concerning Jesus, though he knew only the baptism of John. ²⁶ He began to speak boldly in the synagogue; but when Priscilla and Aquila heard him, they took him and expounded to him the way of God more accurately. ²⁷ And when he wished to cross to Achaia, the brethren encouraged him, and wrote to the disciples to receive him. When he arrived, he greatly helped those who through grace had believed, ²⁸ for he powerfully confuted the Jews in public, showing by the scriptures that the Christ was Jesus.

Apollos was from Alexandria in Egypt, a renowned center of learning in the ancient world. Alexandrians esteemed wisdom, knowledge, and the ability to persuade others to change their point of view. The Jewish scholars from Alexandria took pride in their skills in allegory, of finding hidden meaning in the ancient scriptures. It is likely that in this context, Apollos would have been particularly adept at recognizing how the Old Testament constantly pointed to Jesus the Messiah in hidden ways. This background may also have prepared him to teach "accurately about the things concerning Jesus, through he knew only the baptism of John" (Acts 18:25).

When Priscilla and Aquila heard Apollos preach in the synagogue, they recognized him to be a man of fervor and ability, but one who did not as yet know the fullness of the truth. Seeing that he had great potential to serve God, they took it upon themselves to teach him more fully (Acts 18:26). They invited him to their home and instructed him in the fullness of the Christian faith so that he might be more effective in doing God's work.

Priscilla and Aquila provide us with an example of what it means to pastor people so that they become more effective instruments in God's service. When they saw the zeal and talent of Apollos, they didn't write him off—even though he lacked the knowledge of some important truths. They recognized the importance of teaching and nurturing him, and took the necessary steps to do so in order that his full potential could be realized.

How crucial it is for us to identify, encourage, and care for those around us—both in our families and in our churches—who show talent and interest in serving the Lord. It is in this way that the church grows strong and that the gospel message is spread to all the nations on earth.

As our love for God's plan in Jesus Christ grows, we will see, as did Priscilla and Aquila, the importance of instructing others—or helping them to be instructed—in the full truth of Christianity. Can we keep our eyes open for those around us whom God may be calling to do his work as a lay person, or as a priest or religious? Then can we encourage them and help nurture them as they prepare to work in the vineyard?

"Holy Spirit, help me to recognize those people around me whom God is calling to serve with Jesus in the vineyard. Give me the ability to encourage and nurture them as they set out to become laborers in your harvest."

Acts 19:1-8

[1] While Apollos was at Corinth, Paul passed through the upper country and came to Ephesus. There he found some disciples. [2] And he said to them, "Did you receive the Holy Spirit when you believed?" And they said, "No, we have never even heard that there is a Holy Spirit." [3] And he said, "Into what then were you baptized?" They said, "Into John's baptism." [4] And Paul said, "John baptized with the baptism of repentance, telling the people to believe in the one who was to come after him, that is, Jesus." [5] On hearing this, they were baptized in the name of the Lord Jesus. [6] And when Paul had laid his hands upon them, the Holy Spirit came on them; and they spoke with tongues and prophesied. [7] There were about twelve of them in all. [8] And he entered the synagogue and for three months spoke boldly, arguing and pleading about the kingdom of God. ᕲ

Perhaps Paul noticed that something was lacking in the disciples in the church at Ephesus. So he asked them pointedly: "Did you receive the Holy Spirit when you believed?" (Acts 19:2). When they answered that they had never even heard of the Holy Spirit, Paul took immediate action. As he laid his hands on them, the Holy Spirit came upon them and they spoke in tongues and prophesied (19:3-7).

This narrative points to an important truth we should remember: While we all receive the seed of faith in baptism, we now must nurture the life of Christ in us so that seed might grow and the power of the indwelling Holy Spirit deepen in us. The Ephesians had received the baptism of repentance with a view to faith in Jesus as the Messiah, but they were still unacquainted with the great outpouring of the Holy Spirit and its significance. For a healthy Christian life, it is essential that we be fully conscious that the Holy Spirit dwells in us and that his power manifests itself in our lives.

We may sometimes feel that all we need is a little more earnestness or a little more effort, and our spiritual life will be what it should be. The danger in such an attitude is that it might tend to center on self-improvement and thus trivialize the power of the Holy Spirit in us. By contrast, when we acknowledge that we can achieve nothing on our own and beg the Holy Spirit to enlighten us and empower us to grow in our knowledge and imitation of Christ, then we experience vitality in our spiritual lives. Indeed, that is a role of the Holy Spirit (John 16:13-15).

The Holy Spirit is sent from God. He wants all his people to be empowered by that Spirit. Let us beg the Father to fill us anew with the Spirit and to pour out a Spirit-filled renewal throughout the church.

"Come Holy Spirit, come and from your heavenly home shed a ray of light divine. Come, Father of the poor! Come, source of all our store! Come, within our bosoms shine! O most blessed Light divine. Shine within these hearts of yours, and in our inmost being fill!" (*Pentecost Sequence*).

Acts 19:9-20

[9] But when some were stubborn and disbelieved, speaking evil of the Way before the congregation, he withdrew from them, taking the disciples with him, and argued daily in the hall of Tyrannus. [10] This continued for two years, so that all the residents of Asia heard the word of the Lord, both Jews and Greeks.
[11] And God did extraordinary miracles by the hands of Paul, [12] so that handkerchiefs or aprons were carried away from his body to the sick, and diseases left them and the evil spirits came out of them. [13] Then some of the itinerant Jewish exorcists undertook to pronounce the name of the Lord Jesus over those who had evil spirits, saying, "I adjure you by the Jesus whom Paul preaches." [14] Seven sons of a Jewish

high priest named Sceva were doing this. [15] But the evil spirit answered them, "Jesus I know, and Paul I know; but who are you?" [16] And the man in whom the evil spirit was leaped on them, mastered all of them, and overpowered them, so that they fled out of that house naked and wounded. [17] And this became known to all residents of Ephesus, both Jews and Greeks; and fear fell upon them all; and the name of the Lord Jesus was extolled. [18] Many also of those who were now believers came, confessing and divulging their practices. [19] And a number of those who practiced magic arts brought their books together and burned them in the sight of all; and they counted the value of them and found it came to fifty thousand pieces of silver. [20] So the word of the Lord grew and prevailed mightily. ✍

An ambassador is dispatched to a neighboring country to deliver a message on behalf of the king: "My country is prepared to end trade restrictions if you remove your troops from the border." The ambassador has gone out in the name of the king, with the full authority and backing of the king. The king speaks directly through the ambassador as if he were present. According to commonly accepted international custom, the receiving nation must understand that the ambassador's message has the full weight of the king behind it, and should be given serious consideration.

Whenever evil spirits encountered St. Paul, they encountered an ambassador as well—an ambassador for Jesus Christ. They knew of his loyalty and his love for Jesus, and they knew that he spoke with the full authority of Jesus' name. If Paul said: "In the name of Jesus Christ...," the demons shuddered and did as they were told. With the seven sons of Sceva, however, the demons didn't see any of the marks that distinguish true ambassadors of Jesus. They didn't see holiness, humility, or the real presence of Jesus Christ. Therefore, they were under no obligation to obey these "false" ambassadors, and they turned on them and ran them out of town.

As baptized Christians, we have been given the authority and commission to work as ambassadors for Jesus Christ in the world. The more we ask Jesus to live in our hearts each day, the more evident our ambassadorship will be. Evil spirits will recognize us as Christ's ambassadors, just as they recognized St. Paul. They will be forced by God's universal law to submit to our prayers of deliverance for our family, our friends, and for any situation in the world that we intercede for.

Don't let what happened to the sons of Sceva make you afraid to pray in the name of Jesus! You have been deputized to work for Jesus. As long as you stay close to him each day and allow his Spirit to continue to deliver you from sin and darkness, the demons will recognize Jesus' life in you and flee as you call upon the name of the Lord.

"Holy Spirit, come and bring the life of Jesus into me today. Cleanse me all of sin, and make me more like you. Fill me with the light and the words of Jesus, that I may truly be an ambassador for Christ in the world today."

Acts 19:21-41

[21] Now after these events Paul resolved in the Spirit to pass through Macedonia and Achaia and go to Jerusalem, saying, "After I have been there, I must also see Rome." [22] And having sent into Macedonia two of his helpers, Timothy and Erastus, he himself stayed in Asia for a while. [23] About that time there arose no little stir concerning the Way. [24] For a man named Demetrius, a silversmith, who made silver shrines of Artemis, brought no little business to the craftsmen. [25] These he gathered together,

with the workmen of like occupation, and said, "Men, you know that from this business we have our wealth. [26] And you see and hear that not only at Ephesus but almost throughout all Asia this Paul has persuaded and turned away a considerable company of people, saying that gods made with hands are not gods. [27] And there is danger not only that this trade of ours may come into disrepute but also that the temple of the great goddess Artemis may count for nothing, and that she may even be deposed from her magnificence, she whom all Asia and the world worship."

[28] When they heard this they were enraged, and cried out, "Great is Artemis of the Ephesians!" [29] So the city was filled with the confusion; and they rushed together into the theater, dragging with them Gaius and Aristarchus, Macedonians who were Paul's companions in travel. [30] Paul wished to go in among the crowd, but the disciples would not let him; [31] some of the Asi-archs also, who were friends of his, sent to him and begged him not to venture into the theater. [32] Now some cried one thing, some another; for the assembly was in confusion, and most of them did not know why they had come together. [33] Some of the crowd prompted Alexander, whom the Jews had put forward. And Alexander motioned with his hand, wishing to make a defense to the people. [34] But when they recognized that he was a Jew, for about two hours they all with one voice cried out, "Great is Artemis of the Ephesians!" [35] And when the town clerk had quieted the crowd, he said, "Men of Ephesus, what man is there who does not know that the city of the Ephesians is temple keeper of the great Artemis, and of the sacred stone that fell from the sky? [36] Seeing then that these things cannot be contra-dicted, you ought to be quiet and do nothing rash. [37] For you have brought these men here who are neither sacrilegious nor blasphemers of our goddess. [38] If therefore Demetrius and the craftsmen with him have a complaint against any one, the courts are open, and there are proconsuls; let them bring charges against one another. [39] But if you seek anything further, it shall be settled in the regular assembly. [40] For we are in danger

of being charged with rioting today, there being no cause that we can give to justify this commotion." [41] And when he had said this, he dismissed the assembly.

The crown of Ephesus was its Temple of Artemis, one of the seven wonders of the ancient world. A huge and imposing structure, it was surrounded by 127 marble pillars and featured an altar carved by a famous sculptor. The many visitors who came to see the temple brought home souvenirs made of silver like the ones crafted by Demetrius the silversmith. It was undoubtedly a lucrative business. Any threat to the worship of the goddess Artemis was a threat to the pride of the Ephesians, and to the pockets of its craftsmen. No wonder a riot was ready to erupt!

As Paul sought to enter the fray, however, he was prevented by an unlikely combination of people. In addition to his disciples, some of the Asiarchs—honored officials in the city responsible for organizing the famous Pan-Ionian games—also "begged him not to venture into the theater" (Acts 19:31). Clearly, after two years of preaching in the city of Ephesus, Paul had made friends in high places—Gentiles who were genuinely concerned about his well-being.

Although Paul was a missionary with a religious message, he knew how important it was to cultivate relationships with people from many different backgrounds. Gaining the respect and friendship of various officials in Ephesus meant that he had a chance not only to convert them, but also to protect the emerging church. Paul knew that if this infant community of believers was to survive, he would have to reach out to all types of people, including those in power who could either persecute or protect the church.

We are called to be a light to the world. That means reaching out to those who might not believe in Christ but who are nevertheless made in the image and likeness of God. In their *Pastoral Constitution on the Church in the Modern World*, the fathers of Vatican II wrote: "The Father wills that in all men, we recognize Christ our brother and love him effectively, in word and in deed. By thus giving witness to the truth, we will share with others the mystery of the heavenly Father's love" (*Gaudium et Spes*, 93).

As we extend ourselves outside our parish circles, we can break down walls of prejudice and suspicion that may have existed for generations. When we love others with the love of Christ, we not only expand the kingdom of God, we also help protect it from hatred and prejudice.

"Father, you are the author of all creation, and you love everyone you have created. Shine your light into our hearts, that we may love others with the same all-consuming, unconditional love."

Paul Returns to Jerusalem

ACTS
20:1–21:26

Acts 20:1-16

[1] After the uproar ceased, Paul sent for the disciples and having exhorted them took leave of them and departed for Macedonia. [2] When he had gone through these parts and had given them much encouragement, he came to Greece. [3] There he spent three months, and when a plot was made against him by the Jews as he was about to set sail for Syria, he determined to return through Macedonia. [4] Sopater of Beroea, the son of Pyrrhus, accompanied him; and of the Thessalonians, Aristarchus and Secundus; and Gaius of Derbe, and Timothy; and the Asians, Tychicus and Trophimus. [5] These went on and were waiting for us at Troas, [6] but we sailed away from Philippi after the days of Unleavened Bread, and in five days we came to them at Troas, where we stayed for seven days.

[7] On the first day of the week, when we were gathered together to break bread, Paul talked with them, intending to depart on the morrow; and he prolonged his speech until midnight. [8] There were many lights in the upper chamber where we were gathered. [9] And a young man named Eutychus was sitting in the window. He sank into a deep sleep as Paul talked still longer; and being overcome by sleep, he fell down from the third story and was taken up dead. [10] But Paul went down and bent over him, and embracing him said, "Do not be alarmed, for his life is in him." [11] And when Paul had gone up and had broken bread and eaten, he conversed with them a long while, until daybreak, and so departed. [12] And they took the lad away alive, and were not a little comforted.

[13] But going ahead to the ship, we set sail for Assos, intending to take Paul aboard there; for so he had arranged, intending himself to go by land. [14] And when he met us at Assos, we took him on board and came to Mitylene. [15] And sailing from there we came the following day opposite Chios; the next day we touched at Samos; and the day after that we came to Miletus. [16] For Paul had decided to sail past

Ephesus, so that he might not have to spend time in Asia; for he was hastening to be at Jerusalem, if possible, on the day of Pentecost. ✒

P icture the scene in Troas as Luke describes it. A Christian liturgy goes late into the night. With all the lamps having been lighted, the room is probably warm. And Paul goes on and on! Eventually, a young believer named Eutychus gets so drowsy that he drops off to sleep, and drops right out of the third-story window where he had been sitting. Paul goes outside where the dead boy lies, prays over him, goes back up to the gathering, and continues preaching until dawn. Oh, and by the way, Eutychus is healed and brought back to life.

Luke's description of Paul's long-winded sermon and its sleep-inducing effects offers a touch of humor in the midst of his account of the apostle's missionary journeys. Yet, the fact remains that a young man was raised from the dead! Had this been a rare event in the life of the early church, surely Luke would not have described the scene quite so humorously or offhandedly. It is a testimony to the joyful and power-filled life of the early church that Luke can add humor to so powerful a miracle. Such signs and wonders must have been operating on quite a frequent basis!

Has Jesus changed since then? Not at all. The same Lord is just as available today as he was in the early church. The question really should be turned on us. Have we changed? What do we think about miracles and works of wonder such as the raising of the dead? Doesn't the Holy Spirit dwell in us? Isn't Jesus risen in heaven interceding for us? Shouldn't we be eager to pray and act with confidence? Surely the need for Jesus to work real miracles today through his disciples hasn't diminished. In these days of the "new evangelization," people need to see the power of God demonstrated, and God can use you to do it!

The scene from Troas also teaches us another lesson: Let's not take ourselves too seriously! The less anxious we are in ministering God's power and love, the greater the probability that God will work freely through us! Why? Because we get ourselves and our worries and fears "out of the way" and give more room for God to act in power! Why not ask the Lord to use you to bring about his kingdom in a joyful and power-filled way?

"Holy Spirit, give me confident faith and a lighthearted reliance upon you. As I surrender myself to you, empower me to touch others with your love."

Acts 20:17-27

[17] And from Miletus he sent to Ephesus and called to him the elders of the church. [18] And when they came to him, he said to them: "You yourselves know how I lived among you all the time from the first day that I set foot in Asia, [19] serving the Lord with all humility and with tears and with trials which befell me through the plots of the Jews; [20] how I did not shrink from declaring to you anything that was profitable, and teaching you in public and from house to house, [21] testifying both to Jews and to Greeks of repentance to God and of faith in our Lord Jesus Christ. [22] And now, behold, I am going to Jerusalem, bound in the Spirit, not knowing what shall befall me there; [23] except that the Holy Spirit testifies to me in every city that imprisonment and afflictions await me. [24] But I do not account my life of any value nor as precious to myself, if only I may accomplish my course and the ministry which I received from the Lord Jesus, to testify to the gospel of the grace of God. [25] And now, behold, I know that all you among whom I have gone preaching the kingdom will see my face no more. [26] Therefore I testify to you this day that I am innocent of the blood of all of you, [27] for I did not shrink from declaring to you the whole counsel of God."

Paul spent over two years in Ephesus at the beginning of this third missionary journey (between 54 and 57 A.D.) before continuing on to Greece (Acts 19:1-20:1). As he was about to make his way back to Jerusalem at the end of his third journey, he sensed that he would never again see the leaders of the church of Ephesus. Consequently, he arranged to meet them for the last time at the nearby town of Miletus (20:17).

His words on that occasion provide an insight into his heart and mind as God's servant: "I do not account my life of any value nor as precious to myself, if only I may accomplish my course and the ministry which I received from the Lord Jesus, to testify to the gospel of the grace of God" (Acts 20:24). These words were not unlike the ones that Paul addressed to the Philippians: "I count everything as loss because of the surpassing worth of knowing Christ Jesus my Lord." (Philippians 3:8).

Paul's love of Jesus is evident in his words. The things of the earth were of little importance to him in light of what he had come to know and experience of the heavenly kingdom. It was this heavenly vision that spurred Paul on, despite the trials, hardships, and dangers. He knew that Jesus had been faithful to his promise to send the Holy Spirit to reveal all things concerning God (John 16:5-16). God is faithful to that promise even to our day. It is a promise in which we must trust.

What must we do to know Christ and to burn with love for him? We need to open our hearts to him. We can kneel before the cross and thank Jesus for the salvation he has accomplished. As we do this, we can raise our hearts and minds to consider all we know of God's heavenly kingdom, and we can ask the Spirit of God to teach us even more about the heavenly realities. Let us ask the Spirit to come to us and give us a burning love for Jesus and the desire to serve him.

"Come, Holy Spirit, fill the hearts of your faithful and kindle in them the fire of your love. Send forth your Spirit and they shall be created; and you shall renew the face of the earth."

Acts 20:28-38

28 "Take heed to yourselves and to all the flock, in which the Holy Spirit has made you overseers, to care for the church of the Lord which he obtained with the blood of his own Son. 29 I know that after my departure fierce wolves will come in among you, not sparing the flock; 30 and from among your own selves will arise men speaking perverse things, to draw away the disciples after them. 31 Therefore be alert, remembering that for three years I did not cease night or day to admonish every one with tears.

32 "And now I commend you to God and to the word of his grace, which is able to build you up and to give you the inheritance among all those who are sanctified. 33 I coveted no one's silver or gold or apparel. 34 You yourselves know that these hands ministered to my necessities, and to those who were with me. 35 In all things I have shown you that by so toiling one must help the weak, remembering the words of the Lord Jesus, how he said, 'It is more blessed to give than to receive.' "

36 And when he had spoken thus, he knelt down and prayed with them all. 37 And they all wept and embraced Paul and kissed him, 38 sorrowing most of all because of the word he had spoken, that they should see his face no more. And they brought him to the ship.

A group of youngsters was busily engaged trying to climb up a twenty-foot rope—with varying degrees of success. Most of the children were barely able to make it halfway. Only one managed to get all the way to the top. When asked how he had done it, he said that he kept reminding himself not to look down. Because he was determined to reach his goal, he did not let the height frighten or discourage him.

This same principle was evident in Paul's farewell to the Ephesian leaders. He implored them to be on guard and always to look heavenward to the reality of their life in Christ. He realized that after he was gone, "fierce wolves will come in among you, not sparing the flock." Even from their own number would "arise men speaking perverse things, to draw away the disciples after them" (Acts 20:29,30). These impending dangers were clear to Paul, as revealed by his persistent warnings of their coming.

Paul's strong words not only reflect his great love and concern for the early Christians, they also indicate the steps which the leaders of the church in Ephesus had to take if they were not to lose sight of God's truths.

To be "on guard," as Paul advises, is to place the truths of God above all else and to rely on them. This is not only an individual responsibility but a pastoral one as well. Paul can serve as a fine model for Christian leaders today—in parishes and church ministries, in prayer groups and Bible studies, or for parents and teachers.

We need to be alert and to stand firm in faith against the dangers Paul depicted. We must be able to assure those for whom we are responsible that God loves them; that Jesus died for them; that the Holy Spirit dwells within them. The young boy on the rope might have fallen or failed had he given in to fear or lost sight of his goal. If we lose sight of God's truth and God's plan for our lives, we too can fall prey to discouragement, complacency, or confusion, and let fierce wolves come in among us.

Let us continually remind ourselves and one another of the basic truths of our faith, especially when we are faltering. We must be able to say, "my soul rests in God alone" (Psalm 62:1), no matter what the circumstances.

Acts 21:1-14

[1] And when we had parted from them and set sail, we came by a straight course to Cos, and the next day to Rhodes, and from there to Patara. [2] And having found a ship crossing to Phoenicia, we went aboard, and set sail. [3] When we had come in sight of Cyprus, leaving it on the left we sailed to Syria, and landed at Tyre; for there the ship was to unload its cargo. [4] And having sought out the disciples, we stayed there for seven days. Through the Spirit they told Paul not to go on to Jerusalem. [5] And when our days there were ended, we departed and went on our journey; and they all, with wives and children, brought us on our way till we were outside the city; and kneeling down on the beach we prayed and bade one another farewell. [6] Then we went on board the ship, and they returned home. [7] When we had finished the voyage from Tyre, we arrived at Ptolemais; and we greeted the brethren and stayed with them for one day. [8] On the morrow we departed and came to Caesarea; and we entered the house of Philip the evangelist, who was one of the seven, and stayed with him. [9] And he had four unmarried daughters, who prophesied. [10] While we were staying for some days, a prophet named Agabus came down from Judea. [11] And coming to us he took Paul's girdle and bound his own feet and hands, and said, "Thus says the Holy Spirit, 'So shall the Jews at Jerusalem bind the man who owns this girdle and deliver him into the hands of the Gentiles.'" [12] When we heard this, we and the people there begged him not to go up to Jerusalem. [13] Then Paul answered, "What are you doing, weeping and breaking my heart? For I am ready not only to be imprisoned but even to die at Jerusalem for the name of the Lord Jesus." [14] And when he would not be persuaded, we ceased and said, "The will of the Lord be done."

J ust like Jesus, Paul was determined to go to Jerusalem. His companions begged him not to leave—they knew that in Jerusalem, he risked confrontation, conflict, and possibly even death (Acts 21:12). Paul was well aware of the perils he might encounter. His commitment to preaching the gospel involved dangerous consequences. Still, he remained peaceful and resolved to go forward.

Paul's willingness to face the dangers of Jerusalem was due to his hope in Jesus. Aware of the possibility of suffering and loss, he knew his life was of no value if not set apart and consecrated to Jesus. He also knew that his commitment had to produce tangible evidence. Simply talking a good talk wouldn't do. He didn't view his mission through rose-colored glasses, but was filled with the spiritual gift of courage, or fortitude—a gift that was born from his relationship with God.

Just as with Paul, we are called not only to be *saved* by faith, but also to *live* by faith. In both everyday and extraordinary situations, Jesus wants to give us the courage to press on with hope. Whether we are standing up for what we believe in as Christians, speaking out against social and moral issues in our community, or taking an unpopular position in the workplace that won't compromise our integrity, we face the same question: "Am I willing to take risks based on what I believe?" When we realize the answer is "yes," we can respond like Paul's companions: "The Lord's will be done" (Acts 21:14). Then, from a position of faith and trust, we can watch and wait as God demonstrates his power. He is faithful and will not disappoint us.

Living to please God should be the goal of every Christian. Does your faith move you to action? Does your love for Jesus empower you to do the work God calls you to? God is far greater than any situation we face, no matter how difficult it appears. He provides the power to live a life that pleases him, even when things don't go our way. May we seek God, confident that his Spirit will supply us with the courage we need to persevere to the end. May our love for Jesus make us bold and move us beyond fears to announce the gospel with confidence.

"Lord Jesus, I surrender my life to you. My hope and trust in you moves me to service. I am determined to do your will, however great the risks may be."

Acts 21:15-26

[15] After these days we made ready and went up to Jerusalem. [16] And some of the disciples from Caesarea went with us, bringing us to the house of Mnason of Cyprus, an early disciple, with whom we should lodge.
[17] When we had come to Jerusalem, the brethren received us gladly.
[18] On the following day Paul went in with us to James; and all the elders were present. [19] After greeting them, he related one by one the things that God had done among the Gentiles through his ministry. [20] And when they heard it, they glorified God. And they said to him, "You see, brother, how many thousands there are among the Jews of those who have believed; they are all zealous for the law, [21] and they have been told about you that you teach all the Jews who are among the Gentiles to forsake Moses, telling them not to circumcise their children or observe the customs. [22] What then is to be done? They will certainly hear that you have come. [23] Do therefore what we tell you. We have four men who are under a vow; [24] take these men and purify yourself along with them and pay their expenses, so that they may shave their heads. Thus all will know that there is nothing in what they have been told about you but that you yourself live in observance of the law. [25] But as for the Gentiles who have believed, we have sent a letter with our judgment that they should abstain from what has been sacrificed to idols and from blood and from what is strangled and from unchastity." [26] Then Paul took the men, and the next day he purified himself with them and went into the temple, to give notice when the days of purification would be fulfilled and the offering presented for every one of them.

Paul's third missionary journey drew to an end as he was happily received by the elders of the Christian community in Jerusalem. James and the other leaders glorified God as they heard reports of what the Lord had done through Paul's ministry among the Gentiles (Acts 21:17-20). But not all was well: Rumors were circulating around the community that Paul had advised Jewish Christians not to circumcise their children or keep their religious customs (21:20-21). In reality, Paul had only argued that gentile converts to Christianity should not be bound by the Jewish laws.

To assure the community that Paul was not turning the Jewish Christians away from the Law of Moses, the elders in Jerusalem advised him to publicly perform a deed of Jewish piety (Acts 21:23-24). So Paul willingly presented an offering for his Jewish brethren at the temple and carried out a purification ritual himself, showing his observance of Jewish practices (21:26). Paul went to great lengths in order to protect unity among the believers! He gladly became "all things to all people" to win them to salvation in Christ (1 Corinthians 9:20-22).

Since the days of the early church in Jerusalem, preserving unity has been one of the most important goals of Christians—and one of the greatest challenges. Dissension and misunderstandings have repeatedly broken the unity of the body of Christ. But, at the same time, countless believers have made great efforts and sacrifices to bring the divided people of God closer together. Millions of Catholic, Orthodox, and Protestant Christians have interceded, fasted, and joined in prayer, dialogue, and common actions in the name of Christian unity. In his encyclical on Christian unity, Pope John Paul II wrote, "Ecumenical cooperation is a . . . dynamic road to unity. . . . Unity of action leads to the full unity of faith: Through such cooperation, all believers in Christ are able to learn easily how they can understand each other better and esteem each other more, and how the road to the unity of Christians may be made smooth" (*Ut Unum Sint*, 40).

Just as Paul dedicated himself to safeguarding unity and love among the believers in Jerusalem, let us try to the best of our abilities to foster that same unity and love among God's people today. As we listen to the Holy Spirit, he will guide all our efforts to make that road smooth.

"Holy Spirit, bring healing to the broken body of Christ. Restore unity wherever there is division—in our human families, in our church families, and in the entire family of God."

Paul the Prisoner

ACTS
21:27–26:32

Acts 21:27-36

^{27} When the seven days were almost completed, the Jews from Asia, who had seen him in the temple, stirred up all the crowd, and laid hands on him, ^{28} crying out, "Men of Israel, help! This is the man who is teaching men everywhere against the people and the law and this place; moreover he also brought Greeks into the temple, and he has defiled this holy place." ^{29} For they had previously seen Trophimus the Ephesian with him in the city, and they supposed that Paul had brought him into the temple. ^{30} Then all the city was aroused, and the people ran together; they seized Paul and dragged him out of the temple, and at once the gates were shut. ^{31} And as they were trying to kill him, word came to the tribune of the cohort that all Jerusalem was in confusion. ^{32} He at once took soldiers and centurions, and ran down to them; and when they saw the tribune and the soldiers, they stopped beating Paul. ^{33} Then the tribune came up and arrested him, and ordered him to be bound with two chains. He inquired who he was and what he had done. ^{34} Some in the crowd shouted one thing, some another; and as he could not learn the facts because of the uproar, he ordered him to be brought into the barracks. ^{35} And when he came to the steps, he was actually carried by the soldiers because of the violence of the crowd; ^{36} for the mob of the people followed, crying, "Away with him!"

How much rejection can one person endure without becoming bitter or resentful? Throughout his career as a missionary, Paul was stoned, beaten, and falsely accused, and by his own people, no less—the Jews. He narrowly escaped from Damascus with his life. At Antioch, some Jews stirred up persecution and drove him out of their region, while those in Iconium tried to stone him. In Lystra, Paul was actually stoned and left for dead, and in Philippi, he was beaten and imprisoned. Imagine how Paul must have felt to see his people so opposed to everything he stood for!

In one sense, reactions like these in such far-flung places as Iconium and Lystra might be understandable. The Jewish population in many of these outposts was probably quite small, so one might expect its members to hold onto their religious identity with great rigidity. But this passage is placed in Jerusalem, at the very heart of Judaism, and still Paul and his message were rejected. Here among friends where he was molded and trained as a Pharisee himself, he encountered widespread resistance. Paul must have been hurt all the more because he was trying to demonstrate his allegiance to his Jewish brothers and the Law: He had agreed to support and align himself with Jews under a Nazarite vow. Clearly, Paul was not rejecting his heritage, but his opponents were still trying to kill him.

Once an obstacle to the Lord, Paul had become an instrument of God's love to all. And it was by the power of the indwelling Spirit that he was able to continue loving and serving Jesus, even to the point of risking his life for those who rejected him. What a Christlike testimony!

Every servant of God is meant to have a heart like Paul's. Through the power of the Holy Spirit, Jesus wants to form his attitudes in each of us. To those who surrender to him, he gives his compassion and desire to bring others out of bondage and unbelief into his glorious light. Only the Holy Spirit is able to heal us of indifference and judgment. As our hearts are softened by his love we become capable of representing and offering the love of Christ to others. Our hearts begin to ache for others, even for friends and family members, and we desire to become trustworthy instruments in God's hands.

"Lord Jesus, let me see the world with your eyes. Send your Spirit to soften my heart that I might yearn for the transformation of all hearts throughout the world. May my heart be restless until everyone rests in the arms of your loving Father."

Acts 21:37-22:16

³⁷ As Paul was about to be brought into the barracks, he said to the tribune, "May I say something to you?" And he said, "Do you know Greek? ³⁸ Are you not the Egyptian, then, who recently stirred up a revolt and led the four thousand men of the Assassins out into the wilderness?" ³⁹ Paul replied, "I am a Jew, from Tarsus in Cilicia, a citizen of no mean city; I beg you, let me speak to the people." ⁴⁰ And when he had given him leave, Paul, standing on the steps, motioned with his hand to the people; and when there was a great hush, he spoke to them in the Hebrew language, saying:

¹ "Brethren and fathers, hear the defense which I now make before you."

² And when they heard that he addressed them in the Hebrew language, they were the more quiet. And he said:

³ "I am a Jew, born at Tarsus in Cilicia, but brought up in this city at the feet of Gamali-el, educated according to the strict manner of the law of our fathers, being zealous for God as you all are this day. ⁴ I persecuted this Way to the death, binding and delivering to prison both men and women, ⁵ as the high priest and the whole council of elders bear me witness. From them I received letters to the brethren, and I journeyed to Damascus to take those also who were there and bring them in bonds to Jerusalem to be punished.

⁶ "As I made my journey and drew near to Damascus, about noon a great light from heaven suddenly shone about me. ⁷ And I fell to the ground and heard a voice saying to me, 'Saul, Saul, why do you persecute me?' ⁸ And I answered, 'Who are you, Lord?' And he said to me, 'I am Jesus of Nazareth whom you are persecuting.' ⁹ Now those who were with me saw the light but did not hear the voice of the one who was speaking to me. ¹⁰ And I said, 'What shall I do, Lord?' And the Lord said to me, 'Rise, and go into Damascus, and there you will be told all that is appointed for you to do.' ¹¹ And when I could not

see because of the brightness of that light, I was led by the hand by those who were with me, and came into Damascus.

[12] "And one Ananias, a devout man according to the law, well spoken of by all the Jews who lived there, [13] came to me, and standing by me said to me, 'Brother Saul, receive your sight.' And in that very hour I received my sight and saw him. [14] And he said, 'The God of our fathers appointed you to know his will, to see the Just One and to hear a voice from his mouth; [15] for you will be a witness for him to all men of what you have seen and heard. [16] And now why do you wait? Rise and be baptized, and wash away your sins, calling on his name.' "

St. Paul's conversion did more than just change the life of one man. Jesus' words to him gave Paul, and all of us, a marvelous revelation into what it means to be members of his body. According to Acts, Paul testified, "I fell to the ground and heard a voice saying to me, 'Saul, Saul, why do you persecute me?'. . . And he said to me, 'I am Jesus of Nazareth whom you are persecuting' " (Acts 22:7-8).

By asking, "Why do you persecute me?" Jesus was indicating that an attack against any of his loved ones is also an assault against him. We are members of Jesus' body, joined to him in baptism. Nothing happens to one of us that doesn't affect Jesus. No bit of pain or affliction escapes his notice because he participates in it. Jesus feels every sorrow and heartache that we feel because he dwells in us.

We cannot overlook this truth. When others ridicule or attack us for our beliefs, Jesus is one with us. He too is ridiculed and attacked. Similarly, our behavior toward others affects Jesus directly. How can we slander a brother or sister knowing that we are hurting Jesus? How can we tear down fellow members of Christ's body when our destructiveness goes directly against the heart of Jesus? Even when we feel we have a "just cause," our response must always be tempered by our shared union in Christ.

Let us never be motivated by bitterness, resentment, envy, or revenge. Disputes sometimes arise wherever fallen humans live together—among spouses and family members, amid neighborhoods and parishes, and between Christians of different denominations. Yet, by faith, we know that no situation is irreconcilable if we accept God's love poured into our hearts through his Holy Spirit. Even Paul, a persecutor of Christians, eventually dedicated his life to Jesus. If we honor the body of Christ with Paul, imagine the effect of our unity on the world—the power of Christ Incarnate in our midst.

"Jesus, we ask forgiveness for the times we've hurt you by our lack of charity toward the fellow members of your body. Bring us together as the one body you long for—one church, your bride."

Acts 22:17–29

[17] "When I had returned to Jerusalem and was praying in the temple, I fell into a trance [18]and saw him saying to me, 'Make haste and get quickly out of Jerusalem, because they will not accept your testimony about me.' [19] And I said, 'Lord, they themselves know that in every synagogue I imprisoned and beat those who believed in thee. [20] And when the blood of Stephen thy witness was shed, I also was standing by and approving, and keeping the garments of those who killed him.' [21] And he said to me, 'Depart; for I will send you far away to the Gentiles.' "

[22] Up to this word they listened to him; then they lifted up their voices and said, "Away with such a fellow from the earth! For he ought not to live." [23] And as they cried out and waved their garments and threw dust into the air, [24] the tribune commanded him to be brought into the barracks, and ordered him to be examined by scourging, to find out why they shouted thus against him. [25] But when they had tied him up

with the thongs, Paul said to the centurion who was standing by, "Is it lawful for you to scourge a man who is a Roman citizen, and uncondemned?" [26] When the centurion heard that, he went to the tribune and said to him, "What are you about to do? For this man is a Roman citizen." [27] So the tribune came and said to him, "Tell me, are you a Roman citizen?" And he said, "Yes." [28] The tribune answered, "I bought this citizenship for a large sum." Paul said, "But I was born a citizen." [29] So those who were about to examine him withdrew from him instantly; and the tribune also was afraid, for he realized that Paul was a Roman citizen and that he had bound him.

Paul became all things to all people in order that he might win some to Christ. To the Jews, he spoke Hebrew and they listened intently. To the Roman soldiers, he claimed citizenship and they immediately changed their course of action. This is the virtue of prudence—doing the right thing at the right time for the right reasons. Although Paul longed to be with the Lord, he knew God was calling him to preach the gospel. In exercising the virtue of prudence, Paul maximized the opportunities God gave him to witness to the truth.

When Jesus sent out the twelve apostles, he commanded them, saying: "Behold I send you out as sheep in the midst of wolves; so be as wise as serpents and innocent as doves" (Matthew 10:16). The apostles were to be ready, gentle, and above all prudent. Prudence is a virtue that is often misunderstood. It does not mean being cautious or slow to move. Sometimes the prudent thing to do is risky or impulsive. St. Paul provides a clear example of what it means to exercise prudence, particularly as he proclaims the gospel in an apathetic and hostile environment.

The challenges we face when it comes to evangelization also require prudence. We too must be wise in our efforts to take the gospel into apathetic and hostile territories. But God is on our side. He will grant us the wisdom we need. Furthermore, God desires that all be saved and come to the knowledge of truth. In fact, the Lord passionately knows and loves all people. Ever since they were conceived, Christ has been knocking on the door of their hearts, and he will continue knocking until they answer his call.

Evangelization means filling the needs of people. Some suffer from lack of food, clothing, or shelter. You can do something about that! Others suffer from loneliness, isolation, and oppression. You can do something about that! And, everyone who does not know Christ suffers from spiritual poverty. You can do something about that! In all these things, let your love of Christ compel you to act. Be docile to his Spirit, and move with wisdom and prudence, always making friends—not enemies—for the sake of the gospel. Above all be open, creative, and joyful as you go about winning others to Christ.

"Lord, I see the needs all around me, and I am overwhelmed. Lead me into the way you want me to go. Give me practical insight as to how I may reveal your goodness and love to those around me. Use me, Lord. I am here."

Acts 22:30-23:11

[30] But on the morrow, desiring to know the real reason why the Jews accused him, he unbound him, and commanded the chief priests and all the council to meet, and he brought Paul down and set him before them.
[1] And Paul, looking intently at the council, said, "Brethren, I have lived before God in all good conscience up to this day." [2] And the high priest Ananias commanded those who stood by him to strike him on the mouth. [3] Then Paul said to him, "God shall strike you, you whitewashed

wall! Are you sitting to judge me according to the law, and yet contrary to the law you order me to be struck?" [4] Those who stood by said, "Would you revile God's high priest?" [5] And Paul said, "I did not know, brethren, that he was the high priest; for it is written, 'You shall not speak evil of a ruler of your people.' "

[6] But when Paul perceived that one part were Sadducees and the other Pharisees, he cried out in the council, "Brethren, I am a Pharisee, a son of Pharisees; with respect to the hope and the resurrection of the dead I am on trial." [7] And when he had said this, a dissension arose between the Pharisees and the Sadducees; and the assembly was divided.

[8] For the Sadducees say that there is no resurrection, nor angel, nor spirit; but the Pharisees acknowledge them all. [9] Then a great clamor arose; and some of the scribes of the Pharisees' party stood up and contended, "We find nothing wrong in this man. What if a spirit or an angel spoke to him?" [10] And when the dissension became violent, the tribune, afraid that Paul would be torn in pieces by them, commanded the soldiers to go down and take him by force from among them and bring him into the barracks.

[11] The following night the Lord stood by him and said, "Take courage, for as you have testified about me at Jerusalem, so you must bear witness also at Rome."

Paul fearlessly proclaimed once again his belief in the risen Christ—this time before the Sanhedrin—and he was almost killed in the riot that broke out. That night, the Lord came to him and told him to take courage (Acts 23:10-11). In each difficult situation that Paul encountered, the Holy Spirit helped him, giving him direction, encouragement, and strength. Consequently, regardless of the dangers he confronted, Paul strove to remain steadfast in his faith.

Paul's courage, which flowed from his openness to the Spirit, is a model for us as well. The *Catechism of the Catholic Church* teaches that the gift of courage (or fortitude) is part of every Christian's heritage, something we can all experience and strengthen as we grow in our faith:

> Fortitude is the moral virtue that ensures firmness in difficulties and constancy in the pursuit of the good. . . . The virtue of fortitude enables one to conquer fear, even fear of death, and to face trials and persecutions. It disposes one even to renounce and sacrifice his life in defense of a just cause. (CCC, 1808)

Whether we realize it or not, we too are on trial each day for our hope in the resurrection. Like Paul, we can also persevere in our faith with joyful hope, a hope that will never disappoint us, because "God's love has been poured out into our hearts through the Holy Spirit which has been given to us" (Romans 5:5).

Our courage and our hope are not based on how we feel or whether circumstances are in our favor. Rather, they come from the sure foundation of Jesus' victory over sin and death and his great love for us. It is our faith and trust in the Spirit of Christ within us that will win us the victory as we stand firm in hope: "Anyone who is interiorly united to the Son of the living God will also bear his image outwardly through continuous exercise of heroic virtue, especially patient courage that cannot be conquered secretly or openly" (*The Letters of St. Paul of the Cross*).

Let us pray that this gift of fortitude will be manifested ever more powerfully in and through us: "Come, O Blessed Spirit of Fortitude, uphold my soul in time of trouble and adversity, sustain my efforts after holiness, strengthen me in my weakness, give me courage against all the assaults of my enemies, that I may never be overcome and separated from you, my God and greatest good" (*Novena to the Holy Spirit*, Fourth Day).

Acts 23:12-35

^{12} When it was day, the Jews made a plot and bound themselves by an oath neither to eat nor drink till they had killed Paul. ^{13} There were more than forty who made this conspiracy. ^{14} And they went to the chief priests and elders, and said, "We have strictly bound ourselves by an oath to taste no food till we have killed Paul. ^{15} You therefore, along with the council, give notice now to the tribune to bring him down to you, as though you were going to determine his case more exactly. And we are ready to kill him before he comes near."
^{16} Now the son of Paul's sister heard of their ambush; so he went and entered the barracks and told Paul. ^{17} And Paul called one of the centurions and said, "Take this young man to the tribune; for he has something to tell him." ^{18} So he took him and brought him to the tribune and said, "Paul the prisoner called me and asked me to bring this young man to you, as he has something to say to you." ^{19} The tribune took him by the hand, and going aside asked him privately, "What is it that you have to tell me?" ^{20} And he said, "The Jews have agreed to ask you to bring Paul down to the council tomorrow, as though they were going to inquire somewhat more closely about him. ^{21} But do not yield to them; for more than forty of their men lie in ambush for him, having bound themselves by an oath neither to eat nor drink till they have killed him; and now they are ready, waiting for the promise from you."

[22] So the tribune dismissed the young man, charging him, "Tell no one that you have informed me of this."

[23] Then he called two of the centurions and said, "At the third hour of the night get ready two hundred soldiers with seventy horsemen and two hundred spearmen to go as far as Caesarea. [24] Also provide mounts for Paul to ride, and bring him safely to Felix the governor." [25] And he wrote a letter to this effect:

[26] "Claudius Lysias to his Excellency the governor Felix, greeting.

[27] This man was seized by the Jews, and was about to be killed by them, when I came upon them with the soldiers and rescued him, having learned that he was a Roman citizen. [28] And desiring to know the charge on which they accused him, I brought him down to their council. [29] I found that he was accused about questions of their law, but charged with nothing deserving death or imprisonment. [30] And when it was disclosed to me that there would be a plot against the man, I sent him to you at once, ordering his accusers also to state before you what they have against him."

[31] So the soldiers, according to their instructions, took Paul and brought him by night to Antipatris. [32] And on the morrow they returned to the barracks, leaving the horsemen to go on with him.

[33] When they came to Caesarea and delivered the letter to the governor, they presented Paul also before him. [34] On reading the letter, he asked to what province he belonged. When he learned that he was from Cilicia [35] he said, "I will hear you when your accusers arrive." And he commanded him to be guarded in Herod's praetorium.

Notice the difference in the way the Gentiles treated Paul compared to his treatment by his own people, the Jews. Jewish hatred of Paul was so strong that it resulted in a plot to kill him. But, when the gentile commander learned of this plot through the providential intervention of Paul's nephew, he went to great lengths to protect Paul from any harm!

It's in the midst of this ironic turn of events that we see God's loving protection and his faithfulness to his promises. God had promised Paul that he would preach the gospel before Gentiles and kings as well as his fellow Jews (Acts 9:15; 22:14-15). What's more, Jesus had appeared to Paul and promised him that he would indeed be able to testify to him in Rome (23:11). Now, through the protection of the Roman army, God was about to bring these promises to pass. Over and over again, God showed Paul how faithful he was to his promises. What he has promised, he will do—often in surprising and unexpected ways. Although the fulfilling of these promises sometimes meant hardship for Paul, not one of his promises fell flat.

God is always faithful. He will always be faithful to his promises to all of his people, every single one of us. Unlike some of our well-intentioned human acquaintances, God can *always* be trusted to do what he has promised. He has the power and wisdom to do so. All people, all nations, indeed all creation is in his loving hands, and he will bring about everything that he intends. Sometimes, the fulfilling of his plans and intentions may involve suffering and hardship, but these can also be opportunities to free us more from our sins and draw us closer to God.

As you reflect on the fulfilling of God's promises in your life, resolve to stand fast in your faith, no matter what purification or trials may come your way. Resolve to trust in him, for he is faithful. His love for you endures forever. God has a wonderful plan for your life, and he has the power and commitment to you to fulfill this plan. Abandon yourself to him, and let him work more powerfully in your life to accomplish his will.

"Jesus, I trust in you. I abandon myself to you. Fulfill your wonderful plan and promises in my life, no matter what the cost. I love you, Jesus."

Acts 24:1-23

[1] And after five days the high priest Ananias came down with some elders and a spokesman, one Tertullus. They laid before the governor their case against Paul; [2] and when he was called, Tertullus began to accuse him, saying:

"Since through you we enjoy much peace, and since by your provision, most excellent Felix, reforms are introduced on behalf of this nation, [3] in every way and everywhere we accept this with all gratitude. [4] But, to detain you no further, I beg you in your kindness to hear us briefly. [5] For we have found this man a pestilent fellow, an agitator among all the Jews throughout the world, and a ringleader of the sect of the Nazarenes. [6] He even tried to profane the temple, but we seized him. [8] By examining him yourself you will be able to learn from him about everything of which we accuse him."

[9] The Jews also joined in the charge, affirming that all this was so.

[10] And when the governor had motioned to him to speak, Paul replied: "Realizing that for many years you have been judge over this nation, I cheerfully make my defense. [11] As you may ascertain, it is not more than twelve days since I went up to worship at Jerusalem; [12] and they did not find me disputing with any one or stirring up a crowd, either in the temple or in the synagogues, or in the city. [13] Neither can they prove to you what they now bring up against me. [14] But this I admit to you, that according to the Way, which they call a sect, I worship the God of our fathers, believing everything laid down by the law or written in the prophets, [15] having a hope in God which these themselves accept, that there will be a resurrection of both the just

and the unjust. [16] So I always take pains to have a clear conscience toward God and toward men. [17] Now after some years I came to bring to my nation alms and offerings. [18] As I was doing this, they found me purified in the temple, without any crowd or tumult. But some Jews from Asia— [19] they ought to be here before you and to make an accusation, if they have anything against me. [20] Or else let these men themselves say what wrongdoing they found when I stood before the council, [21] except this one thing which I cried out while standing among them, 'With respect to the resurrection of the dead I am on trial before you this day.' "

[22] But Felix, having a rather accurate knowledge of the Way, put them off, saying, "When Lysias the tribune comes down, I will decide your case." [23] Then he gave orders to the centurion that he should be kept in custody but should have some liberty, and that none of his friends should be prevented from attending to his needs. ⟡

A ntonius Felix was the procurator—or governor—of Judah, a position that Pontius Pilate held during the time of Jesus. Felix became sole governor of Judah in 52 A.D., and he may have served as something of a co-ruler with the previous procurator of Palestine, Cumanus, from 48-52 A.D. This would help to explain Felix's familiarity with Christianity (the "Way" that Luke refers to in Acts 24:22), and it would also explain Paul's comment that Felix had been a judge over the nation "for many years" (24:10). Now Felix would preside for a short time as judge over Paul and the Jews who accused Paul.

It's interesting to note that while Ananias, the high priest, had a professional attorney to help prosecute his case against Paul (Acts 24:1), Paul himself had no such luxury and had to present his own defense.

Yet Paul really wasn't alone. Just as Jesus had promised (Luke 12:11-12), the Holy Spirit gave Paul the words at his hour of need. And what a defense Paul made! Confidently, boldly, and clearly, Paul set the record straight. He was not a threat to the Roman government. He was merely a faithful Jew who also followed Jesus and his new "Way."

Paul's speech seemed to unnerve Felix. Just as his predecessor Pilate did with Jesus, so Felix did with Paul: He vacillated between pardoning his prisoner and accusing him. Like Pilate, he preferred not to be the one to make the final decision, but waited for other voices to tell him what to do. Undoubtedly, too, Paul's confidence under the anointing of the Holy Spirit must have been very formidable before Felix— the same confidence and boldness that Jesus demonstrated before Pilate.

This, in fact, is at the heart of Luke's point in recounting this mini-trial of Paul: When the Holy Spirit comes in power, he gives light and boldness that can shake up even the rulers of this world. In the end, the case against Paul was delayed, only to be taken up again two years later by another judge (Acts 25:6-12).

We need not fear if we are falsely accused and asked to give an account for our faith in Christ. Jesus' promise of the Holy Spirit in time of need is just as true for us as it was for Paul. Although it may not be easy at times, the best way to answer accusations is to trust in the Lord and try to be as honest and straightforward as possible. The Holy Spirit will provide the words and wisdom that we need. By God's grace, we will be able to respond calmly, clearly, and convincingly. In the end, time will show where wisdom lies. Like Paul—and like Jesus before him— we will be able to give a powerful witness and testimony before others through the Holy Spirit who dwells within us.

"Holy Spirit, give me the wisdom and patience to respond to the accusations and hostility of others. Help me to show the life and love of Jesus to others."

Acts 24:24-27

[24] After some days Felix came with his wife Drusilla, who was a Jewess; and he sent for Paul and heard him speak upon faith in Christ Jesus. [25] And as he argued about justice and self-control and future judgment, Felix was alarmed and said, "Go away for the present; when I have an opportunity I will summon you." [26] At the same time he hoped that money would be given him by Paul. So he sent for him often and conversed with him. [27] But when two years had elapsed, Felix was succeeded by Porcius Festus; and desiring to do the Jews a favor, Felix left Paul in prison.

Paul's first defense before the procurator Felix (Acts 24:10-21) interested this Roman official and made him curious to hear more. At this next audience, Felix brought Drusilla, his Jewish wife, to listen as well. According to the Jewish historian Josephus, Drusilla—the daughter of Herod Agrippa I—had "transgressed the ancestral laws" by leaving her husband, the king of Emesa, and marrying Felix. Therefore, the situation for Paul's message was ripe for the convicting power of the Spirit!

Predictably, Paul didn't flinch from proclaiming the truth of the gospel to Felix and Drusilla with clarity and power. We can also assume that Paul spoke this truth in love. Directing his message to his audience, Paul talked about the need for self-control and the surety of a future judgment! Evidently, these words hit too close to home, and Felix became alarmed and frightened. He quickly dismissed Paul with the vague promise to hear more from him in the future—but it never happened. Felix sought instead to hide from the Spirit's power to detect and root out sin.

Felix's actions can prompt us to examine how we respond when the Holy Spirit begins to uncover sin in our hearts. Essentially, we have two choices. Either we can try to hide from the voice of God, or we can let it come into us more deeply to purify us and lead us to a holier, more joyful, and more peaceful life. God is always out for our best interest. He does not delight in punishing us or destroying us. Quite the contrary, if we experience the Holy Spirit convicting us of sin or urging us to repent, it's only because God wants to free us from everything that hinders our experience of the fullness of his life.

It's not always easy to hear God speak to us about our sin. At times it may even be harder to respond properly when we do hear his voice. But with the help of the Holy Spirit, we can make the adjustments God is asking of us. More than anything else, God wants to teach us how to rely on his Spirit for the power to change. Let's commit ourselves to allowing the Holy Spirit to convict us when necessary, and to do our best to respond obediently and with love to the God who loves us so fully.

"Lord, you know me and you search me. You know everything about me. Come with your loving presence and convict me of my sin. Help me turn from everything that keeps me from you."

Acts 25:1-12

[1] Now when Festus had come into his province, after three days he went up to Jerusalem from Caesarea. [2] And the chief priests and the principal men of the Jews informed him against Paul; and they urged him, [3] asking as a favor to have the man sent to Jerusalem, planning an ambush to kill him on the way. [4] Festus replied that Paul was being kept at Caesarea, and that he himself intended to go there shortly. [5] "So," said he, "let the men of authority among you go down with me, and if there is anything wrong about the man, let them accuse him." [6] When he had stayed among them not more than eight or ten days, he went down to Caesarea; and the next day he took his seat on the

tribunal and ordered Paul to be brought. [7] And when he had come, the Jews who had gone down from Jerusalem stood about him, bringing against him many serious charges which they could not prove. [8] Paul said in his defense, "Neither against the law of the Jews, nor against the temple, nor against Caesar have I offended at all." [9] But Festus, wishing to do the Jews a favor, said to Paul, "Do you wish to go up to Jerusalem, and there be tried on these charges before me?" [10] But Paul said, "I am standing before Caesar's tribunal, where I ought to be tried; to the Jews I have done no wrong, as you know very well. [11] If then I am a wrongdoer, and have committed anything for which I deserve to die, I do not seek to escape death; but if there is nothing in their charges against me, no one can give me up to them. I appeal to Caesar." [12] Then Festus, when he had conferred with his council, answered, "You have appealed to Caesar; to Caesar you shall go."

For more than two years Felix, the Roman governor of Judea, held Paul in custody, currying favor with the Jews who had brought accusations against him (Acts 24:23,27). Even after all this time, Paul's opponents remained intent on killing him (25:3). Then Festus, who succeeded Felix, attempted both to placate the Jewish leaders and to fulfill the requirements of Roman law by suggesting that Paul be tried in a Roman court in Jerusalem (25:9). Sensing danger, Paul exercised his right as a Roman citizen to appeal instead to the emperor's tribunal. Festus was obliged to comply—and consequently Paul entered into another extended period of simply "waiting."

How did Paul, who was so used to being on the go, spend his years of confinement in Caesarea? Most likely, he made use of this time of relative inactivity and quiet to pray, study the Hebrew Scriptures, and keep in touch with the churches he had nurtured before his arrest. In addition, he took advantage of any chance that was offered him—such as his interviews with Felix and with King Agrippa—to preach the gospel. All the interminable wrangling on the part of Paul's captors actually provided him with great opportunities to deepen in his own understanding of the Lord and proclaim the good news. It even became the means by which God's word to Paul at the beginning of his imprisonment—that he would bear witness to Jesus in Rome—would be fulfilled (Acts 23:11).

Paul's peaceful embrace of whatever situation he found himself in—even house arrest and threats against his life—reflects his complete trust in God. He was confident that it was the Lord who was in charge of his circumstances—not human beings. Instead of getting frustrated or discouraged, Paul calmly and effectively made use of apparent setbacks to further God's purposes.

Can we learn to trust God that deeply? Absolutely. How? Just as Paul did—by surrendering our situations, one at a time, into Jesus' hands. As we entrust ourselves daily to Jesus, his love will bear us up and we will experience his protection and guidance all around us.

"Father, I abandon myself to your loving care. Help me to recognize how you are at work in all the circumstances of my life. Use me as your instrument wherever I may find myself."

Acts 25:13-27

[13] Now when some days had passed, Agrippa the king and Bernice arrived at Caesarea to welcome Festus. [14] And as they stayed there many days, Festus laid Paul's case before the king, saying, "There is a man left prisoner by Felix; [15] and when I was at Jerusalem, the chief priests and the elders of the Jews gave information about him, asking for sentence against him. [16] I answered them that it was not the

custom of the Romans to give up any one before the accused met the accusers face to face, and had opportunity to make his defense concerning the charge laid against him. [17] When therefore they came together here, I made no delay, but on the next day took my seat on the tribunal and ordered the man to be brought in. [18] When the accusers stood up, they brought no charge in his case of such evils as I supposed; [19] but they had certain points of dispute with him about their own superstition and about one Jesus, who was dead, but whom Paul asserted to be alive. [20] Being at a loss how to investigate these questions, I asked whether he wished to go to Jerusalem and be tried there regarding them. [21] But when Paul had appealed to be kept in custody for the decision of the emperor, I commanded him to be held until I could send him to Caesar." [22] And Agrippa said to Festus, "I should like to hear the man myself." "Tomorrow," said he, "you shall hear him."

[23] So on the morrow Agrippa and Bernice came with great pomp, and they entered the audience hall with the military tribunes and the prominent men of the city. Then by command of Festus Paul was brought in. [24] And Festus said, "King Agrippa and all who are present with us, you see this man about whom the whole Jewish people petitioned me, both at Jerusalem and here, shouting that he ought not to live any longer. [25] But I found that he had done nothing deserving death; and as he himself appealed to the emperor, I decided to send him. [26] But I have nothing definite to write to my lord about him. Therefore I have brought him before you, and, especially before you, King Agrippa, that, after we have examined him, I may have something to write. [27] For it seems to me unreasonable, in sending a prisoner, not to indicate the charges against him."

As we read about Paul and the events surrounding his trial (Acts 25:13–26:32), we are stirred to admiration for his strong faith, but we may also feel inadequate by contrast. We should realize that in and of himself, Paul was human just like us. His knowledge of God's love, however, was extraordinary, and this enabled him to face suffering fearlessly.

Paul's capacity to endure all things for the sake of the gospel can be understood from Scripture. The Pauline letters frequently speak of our salvation from sin and death and the glorious hope of life with God to which we are called. The second letter to Timothy makes this point: "I was appointed a preacher and apostle and teacher, and therefore I suffer as I do. But I am not ashamed, for I know whom I have believed, and I am sure that he is able to guard until that Day what has been entrusted to me" (2 Timothy 1:11-12).

Paul did not face suffering and persecution so willingly just because he was a good man of noble character. Rather, he knew that God had called him to partake of the glorious inheritance of divine life. He knew that this was an act of God's mercy and love which he did not deserve, but which God graciously gives to his children.

It may be hard for us to accept the need for suffering for the sake of the gospel, but we must remember what lies behind it: "Jesus . . . who for the joy that was set before him endured the cross" (Hebrews 12:2). Paul knew the joy of life with God that is available to all who believe. He longed for all people to come to know and experience this joy.

We too are called to proclaim the truth that Jesus came to give life to the world. Perhaps our trials will not compare with Paul's, but if we decide to follow in the footsteps of Jesus, more than likely we too will experience some form of suffering. Let us pray that the knowledge of God's love will enable us to endure all things for the sake of the gospel of Christ Jesus.

"Lord Jesus, give me the grace to follow you and endure suffering for the sake of the gospel of salvation. May I know the joy that comes from faithfulness to you."

Acts 26:1-23

[1] Agrippa said to Paul, "You have permission to speak for yourself." Then Paul stretched out his hand and made his defense:

[2] "I think myself fortunate that it is before you, King Agrippa, I am to make my defense today against all the accusations of the Jews,

[3] because you are especially familiar with all customs and controversies of the Jews; therefore I beg you to listen to me patiently.

[4] "My manner of life from my youth, spent from the beginning among my own nation and at Jerusalem, is known by all the Jews. [5] They have known for a long time, if they are willing to testify, that according to the strictest party of our religion I have lived as a Pharisee. [6] And now I stand here on trial for hope in the promise made by God to our fathers, [7] to which our twelve tribes hope to attain, as they earnestly worship night and day. And for this hope I am accused by Jews, O king! [8] Why is it thought incredible by any of you that God raises the dead?

[9] "I myself was convinced that I ought to do many things in opposing the name of Jesus of Nazareth. [10] And I did so in Jerusalem; I not only shut up many of the saints in prison, by authority from the chief priests, but when they were put to death I cast my vote against them. [11] And I punished them often in all the synagogues and tried to make them blaspheme; and in raging fury against them, I persecuted them even to foreign cities.

[12] "Thus I journeyed to Damascus with the authority and commission of the chief priests. [13] At midday, O king, I saw on the way a light from heaven, brighter than the sun, shining round me and those who journeyed with me. [14] And when we had all fallen to the ground, I heard a voice saying to me in the Hebrew language, 'Saul, Saul, why do you persecute me? It hurts you to kick against the goads.' [15] And I said, 'Who are you, Lord?' And the Lord said, 'I am Jesus whom you are persecuting. [16] But rise and stand upon your feet; for I have appeared to you for this purpose, to appoint you to serve and bear witness to the

things in which you have seen me and to those in which I will appear to you, [17] delivering you from the people and from the Gentiles–to whom I send you [18] to open their eyes, that they may turn from darkness to light and from the power of Satan to God, that they may receive forgiveness of sins and a place among those who are sanctified by faith in me.'
[19] "Wherefore, O King Agrippa, I was not disobedient to the heavenly vision, [20] but declared first to those at Damascus, then at Jerusalem and throughout all the country of Judea, and also to the Gentiles, that they should repent and turn to God and perform deeds worthy of their repentance. [21] For this reason the Jews seized me in the temple and tried to kill me. [22] To this day I have had the help that comes from God, and so I stand here testifying both to small and great, saying nothing but what the prophets and Moses said would come to pass: [23] that the Christ must suffer, and that, by being the first to rise from the dead, he would proclaim light both to the people and to the Gentiles."

I was not disobedient to the heavenly vision. (Acts 26:19)

The story of Paul's conversion on the road to Damascus is repeated three times in Acts. Paul's speech before King Agrippa is perhaps his most eloquent defense of the calling he received when the risen Lord appeared to him in a vision. Although he stood accused by his Jewish opponents, Paul was pleased to proclaim the gospel to Agrippa and his audience.

Undoubtedly, Paul had recounted his dramatic conversion numerous times, each time shaping his story to fit his hearers. On this occasion, Paul emphasized that God's promises to Israel find their fulfillment in Jesus, especially in his resurrection from the dead. The hope Paul proclaimed was the same hope that Moses and the prophets foretold, namely that the Messiah would suffer, rise from the dead, and bring light and salvation to Jew and Gentile alike. It was for this hope that Paul was now on trial.

While many Jews believed in a general resurrection from the dead at the end of time, they couldn't accept the resurrection of Jesus or the fact that he was the long-awaited Messiah. Even Paul, as a zealous Pharisee, persecuted many Christians for this belief. It took one brief but dramatic encounter for Paul to change his mind, and the entire course of his life! And it was this revelation of the resurrection that led Paul not only to conversion, but also to accept Jesus' call to preach the gospel to the Gentiles. As Paul himself confessed, he "was not disobedient to the heavenly vision" (Acts 26:19).

Do you know the promise of resurrection? Do you know that in Christ Jesus your life is very safe, and that you're destined for a glorious life in which you will reign with him? Do you know that you can begin to experience this resurrection life here and now? That you can be raised up above the worries of a life that sees no hope? That you can walk in the power of the Spirit? It was this conviction that kept Paul faithful to the calling God had for him, and the same can happen for us.

The hope of the resurrection is not just some vague hope that we will come back to life after a painful death and a time of darkness. There will never be a moment that Jesus will abandon us. There will never be a moment that heaven is closed to us. There will never be a moment when the Holy Spirit is not working in us to make us more like Jesus.

"Lord Jesus, I praise you for your victory over sin and death. You give me the hope of everlasting life and the joy of unending bliss with you and the Father forever."

Acts 26:24-32

[24] And as he thus made his defense, Festus said with a loud voice, "Paul, you are mad; your great learning is turning you mad." [25] But Paul said, "I am not mad, most excellent Festus, but I am speaking the sober truth. [26] For the king knows about these things, and to him I speak freely; for I am persuaded that none of these things has escaped his notice, for this was not done in a corner. [27] King Agrippa, do you believe the prophets? I know that you believe." [28] And Agrippa said to Paul, "In a short time you think to make me a Christian!" [29] And Paul said, "Whether short or long, I would to God that not only you but also all who hear me this day might become such as I am—except for these chains."
[30] Then the king rose, and the governor and Bernice and those who were sitting with them; [31] and when they had withdrawn, they said to one another, "This man is doing nothing to deserve death or imprisonment." [32] And Agrippa said to Festus, "This man could have been set free if he had not appealed to Caesar."

In a short time you think to make me a Christian! (Acts 26:28)

King Agrippa, like Lysias (Acts 23:26-29) and Festus (25:24-25) before him, admitted that Paul was innocent of the charges brought against him by his Jewish opponents. The only thing keeping him in chains was the fact that he had appealed to Caesar. Such an appeal was the right of every Roman citizen and had to be granted. Paul was sent to Rome to have his case heard.

Paul must have known that there was nothing Agrippa could do for him, yet he stated his defense and preached the gospel to him anyway, even with a touch of humor. And yet, as persuasive as he may have sounded, Paul simply could not turn King Agrippa's heart to belief in

Jesus. His eloquent defense obviously moved the king, but it wasn't enough. Why?

Paul once wrote that in the work of evangelization, one person may plant, another may water the seed, but it is God who actually makes the seed grow (1 Corinthians 3:6). Paul knew that neither words alone nor human persuasion can change someone's heart. Only God can truly set us free to know the truth, and to love and serve him wholeheartedly. This is why intercession is vital to any attempts at evangelism. It's also why patience, compassion, and even a healthy sense of humor are central attributes of any effective evangelist.

How can anyone draw near to the Lord unless Jesus first draws that person? As the *Catechism of the Catholic Church* teaches, "Faith is a personal act—the free response of the human person to the *initiative of God who reveals himself*. But faith is not an isolated act. No one can believe alone, just as no one can live alone. You have not given yourself faith as you have not given yourself life" (CCC, 166, emphasis added). In his mercy, Jesus offers freedom to everyone who is oppressed by sin and despair. That's why the gospel is called "good news." But Jesus will never force his message or himself on anyone. He respects our freedom to make our own choices. The love of Christ should compel us not only to share with others the saving truth and mercy of God, but to devote ourselves as well to heartfelt intercession for those we are trying to reach.

"Holy Spirit, fill me with your compassion and wisdom so that I may freely share with others the good news of Jesus Christ. Come, Lord, and touch those for whom I am praying. Reveal your love to them and bring them to faith in you."

The Journey to Rome

ACTS
27–28

Acts 27:1-26

[1] And when it was decided that we should sail for Italy, they delivered Paul and some other prisoners to a centurion of the Augustan Cohort, named Julius. [2] And embarking in a ship of Adramyttium, which was about to sail to the ports along the coast of Asia, we put to sea, accompanied by Aristarchus, a Macedonian from Thessalonica. [3] The next day we put in at Sidon; and Julius treated Paul kindly, and gave him leave to go to his friends and be cared for. [4] And putting to sea from there we sailed under the lee of Cyprus, because the winds were against us. [5] And when we had sailed across the sea which is off Cilicia and Pamphylia, we came to Myra in Lycia. [6] There the centurion found a ship of Alexandria sailing for Italy, and put us on board. [7] We sailed slowly for a number of days, and arrived with difficulty off Cnidus, and as the wind did not allow us to go on, we sailed under the lee of Crete off Salmone. [8] Coasting along it with difficulty, we came to a place called Fair Havens, near which was the city of Lasea.
[9] As much time had been lost, and the voyage was already dangerous because the fast had already gone by, Paul advised them, [10] saying, "Sirs, I perceive that the voyage will be with injury and much loss, not only of the cargo and the ship, but also of our lives." [11] But the centurion paid more attention to the captain and to the owner of the ship than to what Paul said. [12] And because the harbor was not suitable to winter in, the majority advised to put to sea from there, on the chance that somehow they could reach Phoenix, a harbor of Crete, looking northeast and southeast, and winter there.
[13] And when the south wind blew gently, supposing that they had obtained their purpose, they weighed anchor and sailed along Crete, close inshore. [14] But soon a tempestuous wind, called the northeaster, struck down from the land; [15] and when the ship was caught and could not face the wind, we gave way to it and were driven. [16] And running under the lee of a small island called Cauda, we managed with

difficulty to secure the boat; [17] after hoisting it up, they took measures to undergird the ship; then, fearing that they should run on the Syrtis, they lowered the gear, and so were driven. [18] As we were violently storm-tossed, they began next day to throw the cargo overboard; [19] and the third day they cast out with their own hands the tackle of the ship. [20] And when neither sun nor stars appeared for many a day, and no small tempest lay on us, all hope of our being saved was at last abandoned.

[21] As they had been long without food, Paul then came forward among them and said, "Men, you should have listened to me, and should not have set sail from Crete and incurred this injury and loss. [22] I now bid you take heart; for there will be no loss of life among you, but only of the ship. [23] For this very night there stood by me an angel of the God to whom I belong and whom I worship, [24] and he said, 'Do not be afraid, Paul; you must stand before Caesar; and lo, God has granted you all those who sail with you.' [25] So take heart, men, for I have faith in God that it will be exactly as I have been told. [26] But we shall have to run on some island."

Do not be afraid, Paul. You must stand before Caesar. (Acts 27:24)

When Paul, the prisoner, set sail from Palestine for Rome under custody, he anticipated danger ahead. Travel by sea was risky that time of year, as autumn was giving way to winter. Being an experienced traveler, Paul advised Julius, the centurion guarding him, that it would be best to spend the winter at the little Mediterranean port town of Fair Havens. His advice, however, went unheeded. Paul didn't try to pressure the authorities to change their minds, even though he was convinced they would run into serious trouble. Instead, he remained patient and calm, knowing that God was ultimately in control.

And just as Paul predicted, the worst possible scenario happened on the high seas. A winter storm raged for many days and battered the ship mercilessly. After the crew had desperately thrown everything overboard, including their provision of food, Paul spoke a prophetic word to reassure them that God would see them through safely despite great odds. Paul knew beyond a doubt that God had a mission for him in Rome. He was not afraid to publicly announce that he had a vision in which an angel said to him: "Do not be afraid, Paul; you must stand before Caesar; and lo, God has granted you all those who sail with you" (Acts 27:24).

Paul met disaster at high sea with calm faith and trust in God's providence. He knew his life was safe in God's hands. Just as Jesus had met his disciples' fear at sea with a reassuring faith, so Paul was confident that God would see him through this trouble. Through prayer he found the strength he needed to turn from despair to hope, and from fear to courage.

We can learn from Paul's example to handle adversity—even disagreements with people in authority—with humble faith and trust in God's wisdom. With the Holy Spirit as our guide and comforter, we can meet any trouble or setback with the same reassuring faith and confidence that God will see us through. He will give us whatever we need to face difficulty with peace, hardship with courage, and fear with faith.

"Heavenly Father, 'my times are in your hand' (Psalm 31:15). Fill me with faith and trust in your providence and give me courage to face every difficulty with peace."

Acts 27:27-44

[27] When the fourteenth night had come, as we were drifting across the sea of Adria, about midnight the sailors suspected that they were nearing land. [28] So they sounded and found twenty fathoms; a little farther on they sounded again and found fifteen fathoms. [29] And

fearing that we might run on the rocks, they let out four anchors from the stern, and prayed for day to come. [30] And as the sailors were seeking to escape from the ship, and had lowered the boat into the sea, under pretense of laying out anchors from the bow, [31] Paul said to the centurion and the soldiers, "Unless these men stay in the ship, you cannot be saved." [32] Then the soldiers cut away the ropes of the boat, and let it go.

[33] As day was about to dawn, Paul urged them all to take some food, saying, "Today is the fourteenth day that you have continued in suspense and without food, having taken nothing. [34] Therefore I urge you to take some food; it will give you strength, since not a hair is to perish from the head of any of you." [35] And when he had said this, he took bread, and giving thanks to God in the presence of all he broke it and began to eat. [36] Then they all were encouraged and ate some food themselves. [37] (We were in all two hundred and seventy-six persons in the ship.) [38] And when they had eaten enough, they lightened the ship, throwing out the wheat into the sea.

[39] Now when it was day, they did not recognize the land, but they noticed a bay with a beach, on which they planned if possible to bring the ship ashore. [40] So they cast off the anchors and left them in the sea, at the same time loosening the ropes that tied the rudders; then hoisting the foresail to the wind they made for the beach. [41] But striking a shoal they ran the vessel aground; the bow stuck and remained immovable, and the stern was broken up by the surf. [42] The soldiers' plan was to kill the prisoners, lest any should swim away and escape; [43] but the centurion, wishing to save Paul, kept them from carrying out their purpose. He ordered those who could swim to throw themselves overboard first and make for the land, [44] and the rest on planks or on pieces of the ship. And so it was that all escaped to land.

Paul's journey to Rome across the Mediterranean was filled with high drama and danger. First the ship was caught in a storm that nearly capsized the boat. Having thrown nearly all their supplies and food overboard, the shipmates endured endless days without food, being driven by the wind. They must have feared for the worst: drowning by shipwreck or a slow death by starvation and dehydration. All eyes looked for any sign of land or help from another vessel.

When the ship's crew ascertained that land was nearby, they tried to slip overboard into the lifeboats. But Paul took command of the situation by urging Julius, the centurion guarding him, to keep everyone on board. Everyone would be needed to work the ship and try to keep it from total destruction. Paul also took the unusual step of urging everyone to take a little food. He knew they would need physical strength to swim ashore if the ship finally did break apart. Throughout this ordeal, Paul seems to have remained clear-headed and peaceful, even calm. And because of his patience and firm hope in God, everyone else was encouraged to stay together and not panic.

When the ship did hit a rock and split apart, the soldiers wanted to kill all the prisoners to prevent their escape. But Julius had grown to respect Paul so much that he forbade them from carrying out their plan. He simply couldn't stand seeing a man as good as Paul killed for so arbitrary a reason. As a result, all the prisoners were saved because of this one man's witness. It was no small miracle that all 276 people aboard made it safely to land, all because one man put his trust in the Lord and did as the Lord bid him.

God wants to strengthen each of us in faith and hope so that we can serve him with confidence and meet any challenge with trust in his help. There is no difficulty, temptation, or obstacle he can't help us to overcome. Our part is to trust in his help and wisdom. Just as he used Paul, God wants to use us to bring his message of hope to others, especially people whose lives are cast adrift by despair and doubt. Ask the Holy Spirit to enliven your faith and to send you to those in need.

"Lord Jesus, fill me with confidence in you. Use me as a channel of your grace and mercy to help those who are most in need of you."

Acts 28:1-10

[1] After we had escaped, we then learned that the island was called Malta. [2] And the natives showed us unusual kindness, for they kindled a fire and welcomed us all, because it had begun to rain and was cold. [3] Paul had gathered a bundle of sticks and put them on the fire, when a viper came out because of the heat and fastened on his hand. [4] When the natives saw the creature hanging from his hand, they said to one another, "No doubt this man is a murderer. Though he has escaped from the sea, justice has not allowed him to live." [5] He, however, shook off the creature into the fire and suffered no harm. [6] They waited, expecting him to swell up or suddenly fall down dead; but when they had waited a long time and saw no misfortune come to him, they changed their minds and said that he was a god.
[7] Now in the neighborhood of that place were lands belonging to the chief man of the island, named Publius, who received us and entertained us hospitably for three days. [8] It happened that the father of Publius lay sick with fever and dysentery; and Paul visited him and prayed, and putting his hands on him healed him. [9] And when this had taken place, the rest of the people on the island who had diseases also came and were cured. [10] They presented many gifts to us; and when we sailed, they put on board whatever we needed.

Have you ever visited a country that is completely unknown to you? You don't know the language. You don't know how to get around. Even common things like how to buy a souvenir suddenly become daunting tasks. At first it may be very exciting, but after awhile it becomes quite fatiguing. You begin to desire the familiarity and comforts of home. Then suddenly you meet a perfect stranger who volunteers to be your guide. He is fluent in the language, knows the customs inside and out, and is very gracious to you as well. His hospitality, so unexpected and so complete, fills you with gratitude. You only hope to have the opportunity to do the same for someone else one day.

How blessed Paul and his companions must have felt to arrive at Malta and receive the "unusual kindness" shown by the natives (Acts 28:2). The Maltese people quickly relieved the physical discomforts of these exhausted and famished strangers. And as a result of their generosity, the natives received blessing upon blessing. They witnessed a miracle as Paul survived a poisonous snake bite. They saw their leader's father receive healing as Paul prayed over him. And then, emboldened by such signs, they brought many others to Paul for prayer and healing. In short, they experienced Jesus! You could also say they received far more than they gave.

Our heavenly Father rejoices when his children extend themselves for the sake of others, especially for those in desperate need. We don't have to wait for tired, hungry missionaries to come to our doorstep. We have the needy right in our midst. They may even be in our own home—an overworked spouse who would like to feel appreciated, a child returning from the "battlefield" of the playground who needs consoling, an aging parent who is longing for company, or a friend who yearns for a listening ear.

Let us open our eyes and hearts to the needs of those around us. May our vision become less introspective and more expanded toward the desires and necessities of others. Practicing acts of kindness and hospitality will bring blessings not only to the one receiving our care, but to us as well. Let us follow the words of Scripture: "Do not neglect to show hospitality, for by doing that some have entertained angels without knowing it" (Hebrews 13:2).

"Father, you have been extremely generous to me. Please send your Spirit to create in me a generous spirit. Help me to be hospitable to everyone you put in my path."

Acts 28:11-15

[11] After three months we set sail in a ship which had wintered in the island, a ship of Alexandria, with the Twin Brothers as figurehead. [12] Putting in at Syracuse, we stayed there for three days. [13] And from there we made a circuit and arrived at Rhegium; and after one day a south wind sprang up, and on the second day we came to Puteoli. [14] There we found brethren, and were invited to stay with them for seven days. And so we came to Rome. [15] And the brethren there, when they heard of us, came as far as the Forum of Appius and Three Taverns to meet us. On seeing them Paul thanked God and took courage.

Paul had been through a harrowing ordeal during his long journey from Jerusalem to Rome. After his presence in the temple sparked a riot that led to his arrest, he spent two uncertain years imprisoned in Caesarea. Then, the actual journey to Italy was interrupted by a dangerous storm at sea and shipwreck on the tiny island of Malta. When he finally did arrive in Rome, Paul was greeted by a group of Christians who had traveled along the great Appian Way, which started at the coast of Italy and ended in Rome. Some had come as far as the Forum of Appius and Three Taverns, a journey of thirty to forty miles likely taken on foot. On seeing their show of support and their obvious devotion to him, "Paul thanked God and took courage" (Acts 28:15).

Even Paul, the great evangelist and missionary who was so close to Jesus, was heartened by the love of his brothers and sisters in Christ! Wherever we are in our walk with the Lord, we all need this kind of love and support. It is part of God's plan to give us Christian fellowship, because it is through these relationships that we grow in Christ. As we encourage one another to follow God's commandments, as we comfort one another in difficult times, as we inspire one another with examples of virtue and holiness, as we support one another even with material needs, we are "Christ" to one another. The refreshment Paul needed to continue his work to build the kingdom, by seeing his brothers and sisters in Christ, is exactly the same kind of refreshment we also need to persevere.

If we have these kinds of relationships with other Christians, then we should do everything we can to treasure and nurture them. Carve out time in your life to lavish on those who are your brothers and sisters in Christ. Invite them to dinner, plan a get-together, call them on the phone, offer to pray with them, seek their wisdom and advice. Celebrate the milestones in your lives together—baptisms, weddings, anniversaries, birthdays. In all these ways, we get a foretaste of what it will be like in heaven as we worship the Lord together and experience more of his grace and peace.

If you don't have close Christian friendships, ask the Lord to give you some. Even one or two others who have made God a priority in their lives can nourish and sustain you on your own walk. As you become active in your parish or join a prayer or Bible study group, you will be drawn into deeper Christian relationships—and you will begin to attract others to Christ as well.

"Thank you, Jesus, for giving us brothers and sisters who love you. Help us to treasure these relationships and in doing so, to glorify your name."

Acts 28:16-31

[16] And when we came into Rome, Paul was allowed to stay by himself, with the soldier that guarded him.

[17] After three days he called together the local leaders of the Jews; and when they had gathered, he said to them, "Brethren, though I had done nothing against the people or the customs of our fathers, yet I was delivered prisoner from Jerusalem into the hands of the Romans.

[18] When they had examined me, they wished to set me at liberty, because there was no reason for the death penalty in my case. [19] But when the Jews objected, I was compelled to appeal to Caesar—though I had no charge to bring against my nation. [20] For this reason therefore I have asked to see you and speak with you, since it is because of the hope of Israel that I am bound with this chain." [21] And they said to him, "We have received no letters from Judea about you, and none of the brethren coming here has reported or spoken any evil about you. [22] But we desire to hear from you what your views are; for with regard to this sect we know that everywhere it is spoken against."

[23] When they had appointed a day for him, they came to him at his lodging in great numbers. And he expounded the matter to them from morning till evening, testifying to the kingdom of God and trying to convince them about Jesus both from the law of Moses and from the prophets. [24] And some were convinced by what he said, while others disbelieved. [25] So, as they disagreed among themselves, they departed, after Paul had made one statement: "The Holy Spirit was right in saying to your fathers through Isaiah the prophet: [26] 'Go to this people, and say, You shall indeed hear but never understand, and you shall indeed see but never perceive. [27] For this people's heart has grown dull, and their ears are heavy of hearing, and their eyes they have closed; lest they should perceive with their eyes, and hear with their ears, and understand with their heart, and turn for me to heal them.'

[28] Let it be known to you then that this salvation of God has been

sent to the Gentiles; they will listen." [30] And he lived there two whole years at his own expense, and welcomed all who came to him,
[31] preaching the kingdom of God and teaching about the Lord Jesus Christ quite openly and unhindered.

The Book of Acts ends inconclusively. Paul, still under house arrest, uses all of his time and energy to continue his "preaching about the Lord Jesus Christ" (Acts 28:31). Though we certainly would like to know what eventually happened to Paul, Luke isn't interested in telling the story of this one apostle. His story is about Jesus, the Savior, and how the gospel message spread in a miraculous way through the power and under the direction of the Holy Spirit. The Book of Acts opens on the day of Jesus' ascension into heaven, when the risen Christ told his apostles that they would be his witnesses "to the ends of the earth" (1:8). Now, thirty years later, Paul finds himself in the center of the civilized world.

Only three days after arriving in Rome, Paul gathered the local Jewish leaders to tell his story of redemption. In a poignant way, Paul said, "It is because of the hope of Israel that I am bound with this chain" (Acts 28:20). The statement truly reveals the heart of Paul—a man aching for his Jewish brothers and sisters to accept the startling truth about Jesus. After preaching from morning till evening, trying to convince the many Jews who had come to his house, Paul achieved limited success. Some accepted what he said, while others did not (28:24).

Paul did not let this failure stop him, however. As much as he wanted his own people to know the joy of the gospel, Paul was well aware that, ironically enough, the Gentiles would "listen" (Acts 28:28). For at least two years, Paul continued his preaching, welcoming "all who came to him" (28:30). Even the refusal of the new covenant by God's chosen people could not stop the momentum of the gospel. God's promise of new life in Christ would be fulfilled, and Paul would not allow his own disappointment to discourage him. He knew that God's purposes could not be thwarted—and that his plans are often beyond our own limited minds to understand.

God's plans for our own lives are not always what we might desire. And yet, as the Book of Acts illustrates so clearly, his purposes are grander than we can imagine. How could the apostles have guessed that even though Jesus would not walk the earth with them any longer, the Holy Spirit would come to fill them with such boldness and zeal? How could they have imagined that Stephen's death and the persecution that followed would result in the spread of the gospel to more distant lands? How could have they known, in advance, that Cornelius would receive the Holy Spirit—even though he was not a Jew? Or that Paul, on trial on trumped-up charges, would take the gospel all the way to Rome? God's purpose is in everything that happens—even when we are unaware of it at the time.

We can use the Book of Acts as a reminder of this truth. God truly does work in mysterious ways sometimes, but he always has our salvation in mind. In every age and in all places on earth, he wants to bring all people to himself. Let us put our own doubts and disappointments aside, and cooperate with God's timing and plans. His ways are not always our ways, but his purposes are beyond question. He desires that we win the prize—of life with him forever.

"Father, you are all knowing and all loving. Your Son suffered and died for our sins, so they we might be made sinless. You sent your apostles over all the earth to establish your bride, the church. We trust in your plan for our lives."

Other Resources From The Word Among Us Press

The New Testament Devotional Commentary Series:
Matthew: A Devotional Commentary
Mark: A Devotional Commentary
Luke: A Devotional Commentary
John: A Devotional Commentary
Leo Zanchettin, General Editor

Enjoy praying through the gospels with commentaries that include each passage of Scripture with a faith-filled meditation.

The Wisdom Series:
Love Songs: Wisdom from Saint Bernard of Clairvaux
Live Jesus! Wisdom from Saints Francis de Sales and Jane de Chantal
A Radical Love: Wisdom from Dorothy Day
My Heart Speaks: Wisdom from Pope John XXIII
Welcoming the New Millennium: Wisdom from Pope John II
Touching the Risen Christ: Wisdom from The Fathers
Walking with the Father: Wisdom from Brother Lawrence
Hold Fast to God: Wisdom from The Early Church

These popular books include short biographies of the authors and selections from their writings grouped around themes such as prayer, forgiveness, and mercy.

Books on Saints:
A Great Cloud of Witnesses: The Stories of 16 Saints and Christian Heroes by Leo Zanchettin and Patricia Mitchell

I Have Called you by Name: The Stories of 16 Saints and Christian Heroes by Patricia Mitchell

Other Popular Resources:
God Alone: Stories of the Power of Faith
Twenty-eight real life stories that celebrate God's unconditional love.

Signposts: How To Be a Catholic Man in the World Today
By Bill Bawden and Tim Sullivan
Fifty-two discussion plans offer men the opportunity to grow in their faith.

To Order call 1-800-775-9673
or order online at www.wau.org